TURN IT UP!

MY TIME MAKING HIT RECORDS IN THE GLORY DAYS OF ROCK MUSIC

TOM WERMAN

TURN IT UP!
MY TIME MAKING HIT RECORDS
IN THE GLORY DAYS OF ROCK MUSIC
TOM WERMAN

A Jawbone book
First edition 2023
Published in the UK and the USA by
Jawbone Press
Office G1
141–157 Acre Lane
London SW2 5UA
England
www.jawbonepress.com

ISBN 978-1-911036-34-0

Volume copyright © 2023 Outline Press Ltd. Text copyright © Tom Werman. All rights reserved. No part of this book covered by the copyrights hereon may be reproduced or copied in any manner whatsoever without written permission, except in the case of brief quotations embodied in articles or reviews where the source should be made clear. For more information contact the publishers.

Unless otherwise noted, the photographs in this book are from the author's archives. If you feel there has been a mistaken attribution, please contact the publishers.

Printed by Short Run Press, Exeter

1 2 3 4 5 27 26 25 24 23

CONTENTS

FOREWORD BY CHARLES KARELIS **5**
PREFACE: 'DUDE, THEY'RE JUNKIES!' **7**
INTRODUCTION: THE GLORY DAYS **11**

SIDE A ROCK'N'ROLL DREAMS
1 PARADISE BY THE PING-PONG TABLE **14**
2 THE BRITISH INVASION **23**
3 THE BURDEN OF PRIVILEGE **32**
4 THE GREAT ESCAPE **36**

SIDE B THE EPIC YEARS
5 THE BEST JOB IN THE WORLD **44**
6 EVERYONE WANTS TO BE AN A&R MAN **58**
7 THE A&R MAN SCORES... AND THE ONES THAT GOT AWAY **65**
8 ABRACADABRA, I'M TED NUGENT'S PRODUCER! **77**
9 BOSTON: THE A&R MAN STEPS IN SHIT **89**
10 LONDON CALLING **93**
11 CHEAP TRICK: A TREAT **98**
12 SO, WHAT DOES A PRODUCER ACTUALLY DO? **104**

SIDE C LIFE IN THE FAST LANE
13 WELCOME TO LA **111**
14 (MOLLY) HATCHET JOB **119**
15 THE STUDIO: SANCTUM SANCTORUM **124**
16 THE STIFFS **144**

SIDE D BURNING HOT

17 ELEKTRA: A ROADBLOCK AND A PRODUCTION DEAL **154**
18 MÖTLEY CRÜE: ORGANIZED CHAOS **158**
19 COCAINE (BLINDED BY THE LIGHT) **168**
20 FIGHTING DOKKEN TOOTH AND NAIL **175**
21 HOW I 'DESTROYED' TWISTED SISTER **177**
22 FAMILY MAN **184**
23 ALMOST McCARTNEY, GUNS N' ROSES **188**
24 POISON: NOTHIN' BUT A GOOD TIME **192**

SIDE E BURNING OUT

25 THE DECLINE **198**
26 A RANT: MY DESPERATE ATTEMPT TO CONTINUE **207**
27 THE ROCK STAR AND THE INNKEEPER **217**
28 CRITICAL THOUGHTS, CRITICAL VALUES **222**

AFTERWORD: MAN VS. MACHINE **233**
APPENDIX 1 SELECT DISCOGRAPHY **236**
APPENDIX 2 GREATEST HITS AND MISSES **237**
APPENDIX 3 THE PMRC LETTER **238**
ACKNOWLEDGMENTS **240**

FOREWORD

WHY YOU SHOULD READ THIS BOOK

Tom Werman produced hit records. Lots of them. His records have sold fifty million copies, and while the golden age of hard rock may be over, a surprising number of people still listen to the albums he made with Mötley Crüe, Cheap Trick, Poison, Ted Nugent, Molly Hatchet, Jeff Beck, Twisted Sister, and many fine bands that never achieved rock stardom.

But what are these millions of fans fans of? Mick Jagger gave us his answer back in 1965: 'It's the singer, not the song.' We cherish the product because it connects us with the creative artists who made it.

Mick's stress on connecting with the artist opens the question of just who 'the artist' is. For many savvy rock aficionados, 'the artist' now includes more than the guys with the Stratocasters and the drumsticks in their hands. It includes the producer, who, like the movie director, helps the band define and realize its vision. Whoever dubbed Sir George Martin 'The Fifth Beatle' was expressing this idea.

You won't catch Tom himself arguing for his own status as an artist. He is modest about his contributions. Too modest. Of the more than twenty bands he produced, all but one had their biggest-selling album with him as producer.

So, read this book and let Tom tell you in detail what a music producer actually does—what his art consists of. You will learn about song structure, refining and balancing the instruments' sounds, adding instruments and harmonies. About revising bass lines, vocals, and percussion parts. And above all, about coaxing the best performances out of an often unruly bunch of young musicians. Along the way, you'll learn about many of these unruly young musicians, too.

Then there's Tom's personal story. His personal trajectory takes him from the Ivy League into the drugged-out, money-lined world of rock royalty, and then back to professional obscurity, as the musical tastes of the culture change around him. But Tom's professional story features a seriously successful next chapter in a brand new field, working alongside his wonderful wife Suky. No resting on wilted laurels here. I've known the man for decades. It isn't luck.

CHARLES KARELIS

Dr. Charles Karelis attended school with Tom Werman from the sixth grade through high school. He taught at Williams College and served as president of Colgate University.

PREFACE

'DUDE, THEY'RE JUNKIES!'

'Mötley Crüe bass player Nikki Sixx was pronounced dead from a drug overdose early this morning.'

My bedside clock radio was always tuned to KFWB, the all-news station. The drone of the announcer's voice helped me get to sleep. As I lay there stunned and hoping my ears had deceived me, I flashed back to my recent visit to Nikki's house.

I had made the five-minute ride over to his surprisingly suburban Sherman Oaks home—no rock star castle yet. I walked in to find him on the living room couch next to Vanity, Prince's stunning protégé who had launched her solo recording career a couple of years earlier—and who now may possibly have launched a pretty serious drug habit. She was also charming, well-spoken, and serene. Truly arresting, this girl.

They were sitting close together with Cheshire Cat smiles that I figured must have been prompted by whatever drugs they were doing. By now, Nikki's drug habit was fairly serious, though oddly I had seen no evidence of it when I was with him in the studio, nor did he ever seem obviously high. In the studio, he and Tommy Lee were generally focused and involved.

I was oblivious to Nikki's romance with heroin until one day during the *Girls, Girls, Girls* sessions at One on One studios in North Hollywood, when he arrived at the studio with a shopping bag full of candy bars and poured them out onto the recording console with a laugh. Later on, I asked my engineer Duane Baron what that was all about. Surprised, he looked up at me and exclaimed, 'Dude, they're junkies!' Until then, I'd never known that a sugar craving accompanied a heroin habit. If Tommy—or 'T-Bone'—was involved in this scene, too, it seemed to me that he was just dabbling in it because, as with Nikki, I never saw him visibly under the influence of anything other than Jack Daniels or cocaine (or both).

As I continued to lie there, dumbstruck, I must admit that the next thing to cross my mind was, *What would this mean for me?* If Nikki was dead, it was the end of Mötley Crüe. There would be no more touring, no more rowdy recording sessions, no more decadent record-release parties—and after the label rushed out the predictable 'Greatest All-Time Hits' memorial album, there would certainly be no more Mötley Crüe records without Nikki Sixx.

Girls, Girls, Girls—the third hit album I produced for the band, following *Shout At The Devil* and *Theater Of Pain*—had gone to #2 on the *Billboard* chart, and the Crüe were now huge. They'd become the biggest act I'd ever produced, and I was planning on doing the next album and having it go to #1. The *Girls* LP might have been edged out of the #1 spot by Whitney Houston's *Whitney*, but Mötley had the momentum, the popularity, and the management and label teams to go all the way to the top—and maybe, with some more good songs written by Nikki, they might just stay there for a while.

Damn it, what made this band so incredibly self-destructive?

Right after we entered the studio to record *Shout At The Devil*, Nikki slammed his sports car into a utility pole, and he had to play his bass parts with his arm in a sling. He had reportedly been kicked out of high school and busted for selling drugs, and would be arrested in Japan for throwing a bottle on a train that hit a hapless Japanese gentleman in the head.

Vince Neil, meanwhile, was jailed for driving under the influence and crashing his car, resulting in the death of Hanoi Rocks member Razzle and serious injuries to two other individuals; and even the well-behaved Mick Mars had been arrested in a Denver hotel in a case of mistaken identity. Yet, even as their bad behavior seemed to worsen daily, we had still managed to crank out three huge albums over the last four years.

Now, here I was after decades of dreaming about being a top-drawer record producer, all primed, ready, and eager to hit my stride. What could I possibly do to keep this train rolling? It had been a long slog to get to this point from an obedient, conventional childhood in a Boston suburb—a lot of work, a lot of luck, and a lot of good timing.

And now Nikki had overdosed and killed himself.

* * *

Incredibly, I got a phone call later that same day from the band's accountant, who told me that not only was Nikki alive, but he had checked himself out of the hospital and returned home! I called him to see how he was doing, and he suggested that we go out for sushi at a restaurant in the San Fernando Valley. Talk about resilience...

The myth simply continued to grow. Nikki's experience apparently inspired all four band members to change their ways, get sober, become a fitness SWAT team—and to find a new producer. After three projects with the same producer, it wasn't unusual for a band to choose a new direction. I was disappointed, but Bob Rock did a great job on their next album; until then, I had always produced every one of my bands' biggest-selling albums, but the sales of *Dr. Feelgood* eclipsed *Girls, Girls, Girls* by at least a million.

In the end, though, I realized that I was both fortunate and happy to have been part of the Mötley Crüe legend. I have more to say about the Crüe later, but that morning I reflected on what a long, unconventional, and bumpy road I had traveled before completing the first half of my life's journey—from a suburban Boston public school through a starchy New England prep school, on to two degrees at an Ivy League university, followed by an unpleasant first job, a move into rock'n'roll talent scouting, on to producing hard rock record albums, and finally working side by side with four of the kind of rock'n'roll animals that I had heard about but never before encountered. Decades before, who would have known that someday my immediate future would depend on the recreational indulgences of a rock band's bass player?

INTRODUCTION

THE GLORY DAYS

Music pushes our emotional buttons. Consider The Who's 'Won't Get Fooled Again,' the boys' choir at the end of the Stones' 'You Can't Always Get What You Want,' the guitar solo at the end of Tom Petty's 'Runnin' Down A Dream,' the Hammond B3 organ section between Boston's 'Foreplay' and 'Long Time,' John Lennon's 'Imagine,' Ministry's 'Jesus Built My Hotrod,' ZZ Top's 'La Grange,' the theme from Aaron Sorkin's short-lived TV series *The Newsroom*...

For me, the 'glory days' of rock'n'roll extended from the mid 1950s to the early 1990s. These years provided a virtual cornucopia of songs that colored and enriched our young lives. The guitar-driven music inspired and empowered us, and I was fortunate enough to be there when Elvis appeared—and fortunate enough to become totally immersed in popular music for the next four decades.

In the past few years, interest in the music of the 60s, 70s, and 80s has grown dramatically, and the audience for classic rock now includes those from ages fifteen to eighty. I began doing an increasing number of podcasts and interviews, and I was asked to write eighteen episodes for a popular blog. People wanted information about all aspects of this unique musical period. Seeing this, I sat down to write about what I consider to be the most musically creative stretch in the last century, and about my journey through it; about how major record labels operated, about how we discovered and recorded the acts, and about who the rock stars I worked with and met along the way really were. It was a very special time for music, and I suspect this is why it's earned the label 'classic.'

Since rock'n'roll was born with my generation, I never imagined that someday it would be regarded as *art*, or that we would be in a position to recall it or relive it. I find much of the music of the new millennium annoyingly perfect. We may never hear a vocalist hit a bad note again, and the drums will always be in time, with every snare hit sounding exactly like all the ones that preceded and followed it, because they really *are* all the same digitally reproduced single snare hit. So I continue to revisit the music of my youth—songs that were created, warts and all, by real people with real instruments in what was arguably the most creative musical period of the twentieth century.

What's become clear is that rock'n'roll defined an era, and that era has passed. There's simply no recorded music as creative or as potent from any other period in the last century, and there was simply no way I could avoid being consumed by it.

SIDE A
ROCK'N'ROLL DREAMS

CHAPTER ONE

PARADISE BY THE PING-PONG TABLE

In 1955, Newton, Massachusetts, was the perfect American suburb. I rode my bike to school and left it unlocked in the bike rack; when we were dismissed at three o'clock, the bike was still there, untouched. Wooded tracts of land dotted my neighborhood and doors were left unlocked during the day. Ice cream cones, Devil Dogs, and sodas were a dime each and gas was twenty cents a gallon. Ike was in the White House, and it didn't matter too much to Democrats that he was a Republican. American cars were really important to young boys like me, and we could identify every make, model, and year at two hundred yards.

While it was a near-perfect little world, by the time I was in fifth grade I'd encountered the neighborhood bullies. A few of the sixth-grade kids would ambush me on the way home. They dragged me into the woods, kicking and screaming, either because their parents were antisemitic or because I was the tallest kid in my class, or because they were products of fear and ignorance—or a combination of all three.

Eventually, my mother met with the principal and things cooled down, but I developed and nurtured a pool of seething anger that still boils over today whenever I encounter unfair treatment of any kind. People charitably characterized me as 'combative' or 'confrontational,' but the fact is that I'm easily pissed off.

I didn't have smooth relationships with authority figures, and when I found Elvis I quickly embraced the rebellion and anger of rock'n'roll. I was a behavioral challenge to my teachers—I spent hours facing the wall in the corners of my elementary school classrooms—and by the sixth grade, my parents had decided to send me to private school. The unruly behavior didn't stop there, though; I clocked a lot of detention time on Saturday mornings, and I was even suspended from school for a few days in the tenth grade.

Music became a refuge. I'd turn on the radio in my bedroom when I awoke, and at night it would rock me to sleep. My personal pre-Elvis mid-1950s hit parade included 'Doggie In The Window' by Patti Page, Perry Como's 'Don't Let The Stars Get In Your Eyes,' 'That's Amore' by Dean Martin, 'Oh My Papa' by Eddie Fisher, and Mitch Miller's 'Yellow Rose Of Texas.' I absorbed every note and stored every vocal nuance. I didn't try to do this—it just happened. If I liked something I heard, it would be internalized and installed in the jukebox in my brain. To this day, my memory banks are overflowing with masses of useless but treasured musical input.

Dad put a hi-fi in the den so he could enjoy classical music. The turntable came with a fat 45rpm spindle that lay unused until 1956 when I bought my first single—Elvis's 'Milk Cow Blues Boogie.' There were very few record stores at the time, so I bought it at our neighborhood grocery store, and it was the only Elvis record they had in stock. If you wanted a 45rpm single, you went to the record kiosk up front by the cashier and slid the record off the peg.

It cost about seventy-five cents. Almost all 45s were one-sided hits, and the B-side was a throwaway. An early exception was Elvis's 'My Baby Left Me,' the B-side to 'I Want You, I Need You, I Love You.' This two-sided hit made me a lifetime Elvis fan. 'My Baby Left Me' is one of Elvis's lesser-known, underrated gems.

Like many other pop music fans, I was floored by 'Hound Dog' the first time I heard it. I couldn't get enough of it, and I never will. It was explosive—different from anything I'd heard in my young life. I spent hours in the den in front of the antique convex mirror with the eagle on top, lip-synching and air-guitaring to Elvis. I loved the way he casually slurred his lyrics. In 'All Shook Up,' the line '*I'm proud to say that she's my buttercup*' became '*Umpradassaydasheezma ... buducup*'; '*Dancing to the jailhouse rock*' morphed into '*Dana tooda jay—hadara*'; and 'Don't Be Cruel' offered the line '*Don't stop thinking of me,*' which Elvis sculpted into '*Dohstop tha-hankin ah-mee*'—emphasis on '*ah-mee.*'

When The Zombies were inducted into the Rock And Roll Hall Of Fame, lead singer Colin Blunstone had similar praise for 'Hound Dog.' If not a life-changer, it was certainly a major influence on our young minds. Vince Gill once said about music, 'There's something that it does to my DNA that I can't explain.'

What I hear determines how I feel. For me, there's no such thing as background music. If there's music playing, what's in the background is everything else.

At ten years of age, I didn't fully understand the implication of Elvis's hip thrust, but I'd never seen anyone do it before, and I liked it. The bottom and top halves of his body moved in opposite directions, and his arms flailed to the sides; he looked like he was enjoying being electrocuted.

Elvis introduced me to real musical emotion. I got misty over his heartbreaking rendition of 'Old Shep.' I was moved by his songs: they strengthened me and pumped me up. I wanted to be Elvis in the same way I wanted to be George Harrison a decade later. Elvis moved in a way I couldn't possibly move. He looked incredibly cool. He drove girls crazy. His songs were strong, his voice superb, his phrasing perfect, and his pitch was flawless.

And grown-ups hated him.

While my parents regarded rock'n'roll with utter disdain, I didn't actually reject any of their music. I found some of the classical stuff (Mahler) a little boring, but I listened to many of their LPs of Broadway shows and even grew to love some of them (*West Side Story, Carousel, South Pacific, Damn Yankees*). I liked Sinatra's 'Come Fly With Me' and his *Songs For Swingin' Lovers* album.

I did enjoy some classical music very much—especially the weepy, minor-key composers who evoked a sweet sadness in me. When my third-grade teacher played Grieg's *Peer Gynt Suite* in the classroom, it gave me goosebumps. I asked my folks to buy it for me, and I could see they were delighted that I was moved by a piece of classical music. I listened to it so frequently that by the time I was twelve, I could have conducted it.

I've always cherished the surrender to music and to the special emotion that can reduce a listener to tears—an emotion somewhere between grief and elation, a very special breakdown that can be instantly produced by a series of chord changes from an orchestra's string section or a Hammond organ with all the stops pulled out.

Soon after my parents delivered this Grieg composition, their joy turned to disappointment when my fascination with the string section of the Boston Symphony Orchestra turned to a fascination with the section of strings on the Fender Stratocaster electric guitar. In the baby book my mother kept, she wrote, 'Tommy loves music and rocks back and forth, slapping his thighs to keep time.'

I guess they thought this was cute, but not necessarily an indication of any musical aptitude. I had little or no talent for math and science; I needed to be tutored by a Harvard graduate math student in order to pass trigonometry in my senior year of high school, but I was a quicker study in the arts, languages, and music.

I thought little of my ability to say words backward, to correctly spell any word I'd ever seen, or to retain hundreds of guitar solos, note for note, in my head. To this day, I can make a few bucks at a bar by inviting someone to read aloud the entire serial number (twelve characters) from a dollar bill and then watch me recite the whole thing backward. If I succeed, I get the bill. Fortunately, when it came time to choose a profession, I would be able to put this seemingly worthless talent to work—and I managed to avoid the technical side of life by working with a good recording engineer.

* * *

Home on vacation from college one winter, I asked my parents to sit for a few minutes in the living room so I could play them The Beatles' 'She's Leaving Home.' I was always trying to get a little nod of appreciation from them for the music I loved. I asked them how they could possibly say this wasn't art. 'Well dear,' my mother responded, 'we'll see if it stands the test of time.' So far, so good.

Songs like 'The Great Pretender,' 'It's All In The Game,' or 'It's Only Make Believe' made me feel sad and hopelessly romantic. Gogi Grant's 'The Wayward Wind' really put me in the zone, along with the theme from *A Summer Place* or Andy Williams's 'Moon River.' This music transported me.

The songs of my youth are etched in my memory—measure for measure, note for note. Life was divided into two parts—time when music was playing and time when it wasn't. Hearing music made me see and feel in Technicolor; when there was no music playing, life was simply black-and-white.

I wanted to hear pop music all the time; I was delighted with a birthday gift of a clock radio with a timer that would shut the radio off after I fell asleep. In the 50s and early 60s, Boston had a few zany deejays who put together their own playlists; most big cities had deejays with goofy nicknames and big personalities: Boston had Arnie 'Woo Woo' Ginsburg and Joe Smith (who, thirty years later, would hire me as VP of A&R at Elektra Records); New York had Alan Freed, Cousin

Brucie, Murray The K, and Dandy Dan Daniels; and all of America had Wolfman Jack. Some nights in Boston I could even pull in the powerful fifty-thousand-watt signal of Chicago's WLS, which would occasionally air songs I couldn't hear on local stations. There were regional hits in those days—a song that was a big hit in one market, like 'Dirty Water' by the Boston group The Standells, might be only mildly popular in other cities.

I'd lie in bed listening at a low volume so my parents couldn't hear, and I'd fight sleep for as long as I could, enjoying the music in the dark. My mother was appalled by the very same music that thrilled me. I came to realize that music was more important to me than it was to most of my friends, and certainly far more important to me than it was to my friends' parents. I couldn't understand how adults could denigrate, deride, or complain about rock music—I felt sorry for them. I didn't understand how a song that affected me so profoundly could leave them unmoved. They just didn't get it.

* * *

The summer of 1958 was full of great pop hits that I enjoyed in the north shore town of Rockport, Massachusetts. There were also plenty of disposable novelty tunes, like 'The Purple People Eater,' 'Short Shorts,' and 'Beep Beep.' I tried desperately to get in with the local kids, and I kept falling in love with this girl or that girl because I was thirteen, and when you're thirteen and you hear The Everly Brothers' 'Devoted To You'—or 'Susie Darlin'' by Robin Luke, or 'Who's Sorry Now?' by Connie Francis, or especially the signature song of that summer, 'Little Star' by The Elegants—it's just impossible to avoid falling in love. These songs made you *want* to fall in love—you ached for the girl you obsessed over but could never have, and there were several of those for me that summer.

I tried to hang with the townies—the local tough guys who were leaders of the pack and made you earn your way into their circle. The mere presence of these guys was threatening, and the only way to conquer the fear was to win their respect. Fortunately, some of them caddied at the local public golf course, and I was a pretty good caddie. My mom taught me the game when I was nine, and she was an excellent teacher with a poetic golf swing. The caddies spent a lot of time bullshitting in the caddy shack, waiting to go out for a round. If I felt nervous in their company, I needed only to hear Elvis sing 'Trouble' or 'Hardheaded Woman' or Eddie Cochran sing 'Summertime Blues,' or maybe listen to 'The Stroll' or Duane Eddy's 'Rebel Rouser.'

I weaponized these songs—they gave me the kind of confidence that exuded from guys who sported a duck's ass hairdo or wore their garrison belts with the buckle off to the side. Years later, I would draw on this association—this threatening sound—when I remixed songs like Ted Nugent's 'Stranglehold.'

Rock'n'roll made me aggressive. Folk music made me contemplative. Classical music made me cry. The bittersweet strains of Barber's 'Adagio' were emotionally devastating. It was the saddest piece of music I'd ever heard. I still tear up when I hear it. On the other hand, my adrenaline flows when I hear The Who's 'Won't Get Fooled Again' or Zeppelin's 'Immigrant Song.' These songs just pump you up.

Elvis released albums that provided a foundation for my love of rock music. In 1957, artists like Buddy Knox, The Everly Brothers, and Jimmie Rodgers had had several hits, and there were some hit ballads I liked by crooners like Tab Hunter, Perry Como, and Pat Boone, but during that same year, Elvis had four #1 singles, including 'All Shook Up' and 'Jailhouse Rock,' and Elvis's records constituted a category all their own. Next to Pat Boone's pasty-white 'Love Letters In The Sand,' Elvis's hits were raunchy, aggressive, and insolent. They rocked hard.

Where Percy Faith's 'Theme From A Summer Place' produced visions of moonlit nights and sweet romance by the shore, Elvis evoked images of hoods hanging at the drive-in, slicked-back hair, tight denim jeans, and Harleys. Badass dudes.

Around this time, my friends and I started going to make-out parties—usually in the game room downstairs, below the kitchen. The night would begin with the boys on one side of the room and the girls on the other. Maybe we'd throw M&Ms at each other across the room. The guys hung around the turntable, where someone would swear that Gene Vincent's 'Woman Love' (the B-side of 'Be-Bop-A-Lula') contained the lyric *'fuckin' and a-kissin'.'* I insisted that no matter how greasy Gene might be, it had to be *'huggin' and a-kissin',*' and he only wanted us to *think* it wasn't.

The girls would eventually gain control of the Victrola and put on a Johnny Mathis song. Thank you, God. His singing and the accompanying string arrangements were so romantic that you couldn't help falling in love with your dance partner, no matter who she was or what she looked like.

Slow dancing provided one of the very few opportunities to press your entire body against a girl's. Swaying to 'Chances Are' or 'The Twelfth Of Never' on the concrete floor under the dim lights with the colored gels, I simply wanted to ravish the girl in my arms right there between the ping pong table and the oil burner.

At fifteen, I attended a work camp in northern Vermont, where I met a smart city kid from New York named Mike McCarthy. Mike attended a private school in Manhattan, and on his commute to and from Queens, he would stand between the subway cars so he could smoke a Marlboro Red. To me, this was the height of cool. Mike taught me the basic I–IV–V chords on the guitar, and suddenly I was playing songs I heard on the radio—songs by Ricky Nelson or Buddy Holly.

'Peggy Sue' is basically a three-chord song. While I couldn't learn to read or write music, I had a good right wrist and good timing, enabling me to play a solid rhythm guitar.

Until the late 60s, there were two different types of guitar players—lead and rhythm. George was lead; John was rhythm. Stills was lead; Crosby was rhythm. Keith was lead; Brian was rhythm. Then, all of a sudden, everyone was a lead guitarist. Some combined the two: Pete Townshend was a brilliant rhythm player who could play lead as well, but The Who's musical signature was inscribed by Pete's rhythm playing—driven by his right hand rather than his left.

In high school, I discovered folk music and Bo Diddley, and I became devoted to both. *Odetta At The Gate Of Horn*, Josh White, Jim Kweskin's Jug Band, and The Weavers all contributed to my fascination with fretted instruments. Kweskin's dad and my dad were grad-school classmates, so while Jim was attending Boston University, he gave me a few fingerpicking lessons in exchange for some of my mother's home-cooked dinners.

With a thumb pick and two finger picks, I could play a decent 'Freight Train' on an old acoustic guitar I had discovered in my aunt's attic. But it was Bo Diddley who defined the kind of fretted instrument I really wanted to play and how I wanted to play it. I became a rhythm guitarist by default, relying much more on feel than on any musical theory. I never was able to read or write music, but then I've heard that Paul McCartney doesn't read music either. So there.

Suburban life in the 50s was special, and its music would be invaluable in teaching me to help bands craft their music in the recording studio, decades later.

CHAPTER TWO

You can't say enough about The Beatles. Their influence on culture, politics, the media, music, art, sound engineering, fashion, grooming, humor and so much else was far-reaching, timely, and revolutionary. America was in a funk following the Kennedy assassination, baby boomers were going off to college, and along came an unusual and new approach to all aspects of the pop music experience.

When I discovered Elvis, he was easily the coolest guy on the planet. For me, he held that title for about a decade. In 1964, The Beatles raised the cool bar so high that I burned with envy. It got to a point where I didn't just love their music—I ached to *be* a Beatle. I related to them in a way I hadn't related to Elvis.

I was an Ivy League college student living independently in New York City, studying a curriculum designed to make me a creative, successful, and productive member of society, but I believed I could do many things a Beatle could—not as well, of course, but I could still try. I had a great band, I grew my hair, and we embraced dark suits and what came to be called Beatle boots.

I simply couldn't get over The Beatles. I didn't scream, I didn't cry, I didn't hyperventilate or pass out—but I was undeniably obsessed. That fall, I knew there was something special going on when people began referring to the members of The Beatles by their first names only. Their impact dwarfed Elvis's, and I couldn't imagine how anyone or anything could achieve the power and glory of a Beatle. Here was George Harrison, with his charming accent, fine wardrobe, and a voice and a guitar style that were all totally new, and overnight he became the coolest guy in the world. I couldn't possibly imagine that one day I'd actually meet and speak with him.

Many children of the 60s include the first night of three successive *Ed Sullivan* appearances in their collection of indelible events, right along with the assassination of JFK and John Lennon. We remember where we were and how we felt, just as I remember Sullivan himself, hunched over, head wagging from side to side, chastising the audience of screaming teenage girls—'you promised, you promised'—as they raised a window-shattering mob screech, despite the pre-show agreement to be quiet. The audience screamed so loudly that I could hear the band's microphones distort.

'And now, right here on our stage, before we bring out Topo Gigio . . . The Beatles!'

I was playing in a band that year, and when I returned to the Columbia campus from Boston, I suggested to my bandmate, Rick Tyson, that we go down to Penn Station to see The Beatles' train arrive from D.C. for their first New York appearance.

We had gone to Carnegie Hall a couple of weeks earlier to get tickets for their concert. I paid $7.50 for an orchestra seat in row M on the aisle. We chose the late show, correctly thinking that this would diminish the din from the screaming young girls who would be at home in bed by that time.

Hoping to catch a glimpse of the band on their arrival in New York, we boarded the 7th Avenue IRT from the 116th Street station and rode down to the Penn Station stop, where we exited the subway car into a throng of what the news later estimated to be thousands of screaming young girls. Not only were we the only visible males but, at nineteen, we also appeared to be the oldest fans there.

Rick and I didn't care. We knew we had to be there. We'd heard Beatles songs filling the air for weeks and weeks, we'd seen hundreds of photos of them and read thousands of words about them, and we knew that something very important was happening. We made the effort to be there—to go outside of our comfortable campus world to be a part of a historic event. Sinatra and Elvis had inspired wild and enthusiastic crowds of fans, but none of their appearances had ever provoked scenes like the ones The Beatles inspired. We could have felt foolish in the madness of that moment, but it was exciting enough just to be in the same building they were in.

We never did see The Beatles that afternoon, but being in the midst of a vast teeming mass of teenage girls was both exciting and a little uncomfortable. A group scream went up and the crowd surged in one direction, then another scream and a surge the other way. The sweet smell of thousands of frenzied adolescent girls hid the musty odor of Penn Station's train platforms; it was a veritable sea of estrogen, and the noise was almost unbearable.

A few nights later, at Carnegie Hall, we saw—and clearly heard—The Beatles. The younger girls who had been at the early show were, as we suspected, home in bed, and there were folding chairs on either side of the stage to accommodate the overflow audience. Freddy Cannon, Happy Rockefeller, and Lesley Gore were among that identifiable and privileged group onstage.

I'm betting that there are relatively few people in this country who have clearly heard a Beatles performance. But Rick and I did, sitting a mere thirteen rows from the band. They did a brief set—maybe thirty minutes at most. They were powerful, tight, and in tune. This was a killer band in all respects, and for me, they were an enormous inspiration.

What I saw that night was vintage Beatles—the appearance, movements, and sounds that every Beatles tribute band in the last fifty years has tried to duplicate. John with his knees slightly spread, bobbing up and down at the mike and singing with a twinkle in his eye, head tilted back slightly; Paul earnestly singing with eyes wide open, shaking his hair, inscribing little circles with the headstock of his Höfner bass; George a few steps behind them and off to the side, smiling slyly, playing effortlessly and oozing cool; and, of course, Ringo, grinning widely, beating the drums casually but solidly (without looking at them) and bobbing his head back and forth to the beat.

For the next several years, my fellow band members and I did everything we could to channel The Beatles. Affordable quality earphones weren't available at the time, so I'd take my Lafayette Criterion 100-A speakers off the bedroom wall and place them on the bed facing each other. Then I'd smoke a joint, lie on my back, rest my head between the speakers, and listen very, very closely to each new Beatles record via this novel form of open-ear stereo that I had created. Sometimes the whole drum kit would be on one side, or all the vocals on one side—few instruments could actually be heard in both speakers. This afforded great clarity.

Revolver is still my favorite Beatles album—and, as a bonus to me, it was George's breakout album. He'd written three of the best songs on the record—'I Want To Tell You,' 'Taxman,' and 'Love You To.'

I gathered a lot of musical information from *Revolver* that I would go on to use in my career. 'Taxman,' for example, features an actual tambourine part. This wasn't someone randomly shaking a tambourine, as we were used to hearing on pop or folk songs; someone had created an arrangement for the tambourine, with a specific pattern for the verse, another one for the chorus, and so on. (Strangely, a few years later, 'Mean Mr. Mustard' had a tambourine that sounded purposely random. It appears and disappears with no consistency at all.) Inspired by 'Taxman,' I would later provide all the hand percussion (tambourine, maracas, cowbell) and did my own handclaps on all the records I produced—specific parts for specific sections of a song.

In 1965, I paid five dollars to see the first Rolling Stones show in New York, at the Academy Of Music on 14th Street. I remember seeing a photo of Jagger for the first time and thinking to myself, *What a homely, strange face he has.* A few months later, his face no longer appeared strange or homely to me. It was cool and fascinating—and, with the eyeliner, slightly androgynous. The band's music changed the way I saw that face.

At the show, I had to repeatedly ask the girl in front of me to sit down. I was in the second row of the balcony, and she would leap to her feet and wave her arms wildly in the air, trying desperately to catch Mick's eye and maybe be rewarded with his toothy grin. The show was intense. Charlie and Bill looked bored and emotionless; Keith was focused on the neck of his guitar, rarely looking at the audience; Brian wore a sly smile, as if he was in on some kind of secret; and Mick was, of course, Mick. I knew every note of every song, but this was an early learning experience, demonstrating that the live version wasn't an exact reproduction of the recorded one. There were clams, flats and sharps, missed guitar notes—but in the case of the Stones, it was somehow all right.

The Stones played songs like 'Round And Round,' 'It's Alright' (listed on the album jacket as 'I'm Alright'), and 'Little Red Rooster.' When they left the stage after only twenty-five minutes, I was disappointed; when they didn't return for an encore, I felt cheated. Afterward, I was able to find the show's promoter, and I complained to him about the brevity of the set. He politely replied, 'I'd like to help you, lad, but if Mick Jagger wants to play for only twenty-five minutes, there's not much I can do about it.'

This promoter turned out to be Sid Bernstein, a gentleman among music industry jackals who would later put The Beatles in Shea

Stadium. When I started working at Epic Records, seven years after this concert, I'd run into Sid on 6th Avenue from time to time, and he would always spare a few minutes to stop and talk. He always asked how my family was. Sid was one of the most soft-spoken, courteous, and considerate men I ever met in the record industry.

In 1969, I scored two seats from a sidewalk scalper for myself and Suky, whom I had married in 1968, to see the Stones at Madison Square Garden. I paid $18.50 a seat, which was a huge price to pay then. My friends thought I was crazy. As it turned out, the seats were second-row center, and the show was recorded live. I believe much of that show is on side two of *Get Yer Ya-Ya's Out*—most importantly, 'Midnight Rambler,' with Mick Taylor on guitar. Halfway through the tune, the band accelerates from a trot to a gallop, and Taylor plays a marvelous—yet too brief—little guitar solo that I never forgot after I saw him reel it off at the Garden.

The Rolling Stones introduced the possibility of behaving—and creating music—in a manner that was way outside my standard operating zone. Their thorough disregard for convention was remarkable. I think they set an example for the punk musicians who would arrive on the scene a decade later, and who purposely avoided perfection in their performances.

The Stones were highly imperfect—especially compared to The Beatles and other British groups of that era—but the near misses on their records only served to make them more genuine. The punk bands would take this intentional carelessness to an extreme.

That night in the Garden, things got a little out of hand, and when we stood up near the end of the show, people from the rows behind us climbed over the backs of our seats and stood on them. The aisles filled up, and hundreds of people rushed the stage. The meager security staff could barely keep things under control, and we had a tough time keeping our balance and seeing the remainder of the show.

I left the concert feeling a little disillusioned, disturbed by this rude behavior of my generation, but I was bursting with energy, inspired by and infused with the power of what I'd just seen and heard. As with The Beatles, the audience had simply lost it. Thousands of people had risen to their feet, screamed their lungs out, pushed others out of the way, and climbed over others to stand on arena seats that belonged to someone else. This was real rock'n'roll.

* * *

Many of the notable musicians who led the British Invasion were devotees of American blues and later of Motown and American rhythm & blues. Bands like The Rolling Stones and Led Zeppelin simply re-interpreted black blues music for white Americans. Alvin Lee of Ten Years After once said, 'We were recycling American music, and they were calling it the English sound.'

Music is derivative; each generation borrows something from the previous one and modifies it a little, or maybe very little (compare the verse melodies of the Eagles' 'Peaceful Easy Feeling,' for example, with Dylan's 'Blowin' In The Wind').

For such a small country, the United Kingdom—whose population was one third of the USA's—produced a staggering volume of quality rock'n'roll in one decade alone. A generation of British baby boomers had grown up listening to American pop artists, from Elvis to the Everly Brothers, Chuck Berry to The Beach Boys, and now these self-taught British musicians were out of art school, unemployed, and playing in hundreds of bands all over the country.

Before 1964, you could count on one hand the number of pop hits that came to America from the UK. One early hit, 'Rock Island Line' by Lonnie Donegan, was released in 1956. This was one of the first songs that got me to tap my foot and nod my head to the insistent beat. It energized me. As with most other British records of the time, it was nearly impossible to detect an accent (in this case Scottish), so I assumed Lonnie Donegan was one of us. After all, he was singing about an American railway line.

Several other British pop songs made an impact here, including 'I Remember You' by Frank Ifield and 'Bad Boy' by Marty Wilde. I wore that platter out. But aside from these and a handful of other songs that received some airplay in America, there were few British pop hits in the United States until 1964.

I had entered Columbia College in the fall of '63. My senior year in high school had been a pretty good one for American music—'The Locomotion,' 'He's A Rebel,' and 'Green Onions,' plus at least five different hits by The Beach Boys and a few by The Four Seasons—but very little from England. Then, at the start of my freshman year, even as America was just discovering Dylan and Simon & Garfunkel, The Beatles opened the British floodgates, and, for the rest of the decade, it seemed there were relatively few American-made hit records. My college years were lightly seasoned with American acts—The Doors, Simon & Garfunkel, Sonny & Cher, Hendrix, the Airplane, and the Dead—but most of them came well after the start of the British Invasion.

Meanwhile, out of England, a veritable avalanche of great music dominated our airwaves: The Beatles, the Stones, The Who, The Hollies, The Moody Blues, Gerry & The Pacemakers, Peter & Gordon, Donovan, Herman's Hermits, The Yardbirds, Small Faces, The Kinks, Traffic, Cream. It carried on into the 70s with Zeppelin, Bowie, T. Rex, Rod Stewart, Queen, Pink Floyd, Elton John, Mott The Hoople, Fleetwood Mac, Sex Pistols, The Police, Elvis Costello, Ten Years After, The Clash—such an enormous wealth of wonderful rock'n'roll from such a modest population.

Unique songs like 'All The Young Dudes,' 'I'd Love To Change The World,' 'Bang A Gong,' and 'My Generation' defined a whole new approach to songwriting and recording. How does one compare a lyric like '*Messrs. K & H assure the public their production will be second to none,*' or '*They've been some days in preparation, a splendid time is guaranteed for all,*' with '*See the girl with the red dress on... she can do the boogie all night long*'?

The British Invasion made everything from the United Kingdom trendy. The accent, the clothing, the slang—the British had instantly morphed from uptight, formal, and boring to very, very cool. Roger Miller had a hit with a song called 'England Swings.' Gerry & The Pacemakers informed us that the river running through Liverpool was called the Mersey. The Stones revealed that London's Knightsbridge was posh, and Stepney was working class. The Who sketched a colorful description of the mods and the rockers, motor scooters, the importance of zoot suits, and fighting on the beach at Brighton. All of this was new to us.

Some British music fans see the American rock scene in the 60s and 70s as being free, loving, peaceful, and joyous in comparison to the British music scene, which they characterize as more well-behaved and even fashionable. They see American rock festivals as gathering places for free expression, jubilation, and total abandonment, whereas they feel that the British festivals were more subdued. But if that's accurate, at least the Brits can take credit for providing most of the musical fuel for our bacchanalian festivals, parties, and decadent club nights.

CHAPTER THREE

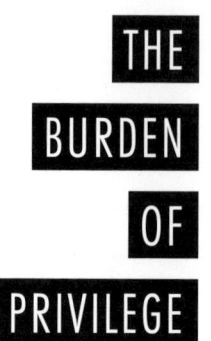

THE BURDEN OF PRIVILEGE

I never wanted to go to business school, but my young life was carefully choreographed by my parents to prepare me to be a captain of industry. Dad went to Harvard Business School, Mom went to Wellesley, and they weren't about to let my New England prep school and Ivy League educations lead to anything but a professional graduate school. Doctor, lawyer, CEO: these were presented to me as my most promising career choices. Every phone call home from college was an opportunity for them to remind me that the guitar was for weekends—a hobby, not a vocation.

It wasn't until October of 1969, when I started my first job, that I realized I had taken a very wrong turn. Even before I collected my MBA, I knew I didn't have the right stuff to be a CEO.

Well-educated kids don't want to disappoint their parents by failing to achieve a prestigious title or a comfy lifestyle. They know that the quickest and safest path to affluence is the path of convention—not the path of risk. After I started my brief, unhappy career in advertising, I realized that less-fortunate kids saw an entertainment career as a ticket to riches and fame; they had nowhere to go but up. Middle- and upper-class kids are far less likely to reach for the brass ring than those from blue-collar backgrounds. Middle-class kids are supposed to be grateful for their parents' investment in their futures—and act accordingly.

My parents' values were traditional, and they wanted me to be well prepared to enter a world they hoped would be just like theirs, or maybe even a little better. Looking back, I see they didn't realize that so many unforeseen cultural changes would create a very wide gap between my generation and theirs. Still, most of my high-school friends stayed in Boston and went into their fathers' businesses, and most of them did very well for themselves.

When I was young, Dad would sometimes take me with him to his office. I think he hoped the vibe would rub off and that I'd eventually want to make the office my home. After all, working in an office was a privilege you *earned*. I would play with the adding machine, and I enjoyed the smell of the mimeograph and the carbon paper—but as soon as I got home, I went into my bedroom and turned on the radio.

We all make poor choices at some point in our lives; for me, attending business school after college was one of these. Up to that point, all of life's choices had been made *for* me, not *by* me. Because of my parents' pressure, I felt obliged to get an MBA.

Enrollment in a master's program also afforded me a deferment from the Vietnam draft. Once I was accepted at Columbia Business School, I was happy to stay in Morningside Heights for another two years, but the school itself was uncomfortable for me, and I felt like a stranger in a strange land.

Coming back from Midtown one evening during my first year at the school, I came upon a large, raucous demonstration in front of the New York Hilton at 52nd Street and 6th Avenue. Secretary Of State Dean Rusk was being honored as 'Humanitarian Of The Year' in the hotel ballroom—at the very height of the Vietnam War, no less. Someone on the scene told me a policeman had been hit in the head by a bottle.

I watched with interest from the corner sidewalk for a minute or so and then, without warning, I received a crushing blow to the top of my head from a three-foot-long oak riot stick (not your ordinary Billy club) and crumpled to the ground. I was immediately surrounded by several cops, so I reflexively curled into a fetal position. They beat me pretty badly, whacking my hands and ribs and jabbing at my groin with their clubs.

After a few seconds I managed to spring to my feet and break through their tight circle, and I ran as fast as I could down 53rd Street toward 5th Avenue. I put my hand on the top of my head, and there was so much blood in my hair that it splashed, dribbling down my forehead into my eyes. Blood in your eye is no fun—it stings.

Very fortunately, several ambulances were standing by, as ordered, waiting to transport civilian casualties to Roosevelt Hospital. Such was the norm at political demonstrations in 60s New York. At the hospital, they met our ambulance with wheelchairs, rolled me in, cleaned me up, shaved my head, put eighteen stitches in my scalp, rolled me back down, and put me in a cab. No questions asked.

The following morning, I arrived all bandaged up at my first class of the day, 'Human Behavior In Organizations.'

'My God,' one of my classmates asked, 'what happened to you?'

I explained the experience to him, and I wasn't surprised to hear him reply, 'What the hell were you doing there anyway?'

Most of the B-school students wore three-piece suits to class and tucked a folded *Wall Street Journal* under their arms. This irritated the hell out of me, but I did make one new friend. After classes, he and I would sometimes go to a movie. One afternoon, we went to see *2001: A Space Odyssey* for the first time, in the original Cinerama format, at the 47th Street Cinerama Theater in Times Square. We smoked a joint on the walk from the subway to the theater, and though our reserved seats were near the middle of the orchestra, we fortunately found two empty seats in the center of the very first row. And there, in seat 101A, I enjoyed a life-changing cinematic experience.

I went on to see *2001* five more times during the summer of 1968. Like many who saw it, I loved the opening scene ('The Dawn Of

Man'), with the ape hurling a bone into the sky, roaring with exultation at having discovered a weapon he could use to crush his enemy's skull. I related to this rage, and later, on occasions, I'd call upon it in the recording studio when I was dialing in a guitar sound. It was my little musical weapon.

In the late 60s, the job market offered MBA students a wide choice. Companies came to interview us right there on campus—if we wanted an interview, we'd simply write our names on a sign-up sheet. There were so many jobs available that we could have stood on the steps of the school and told the corporate recruiters to get in line, take a number, and give us their best offers.

I signed up for interviews with several companies, including Grey Advertising, Procter & Gamble, and CBS Records. I enjoyed meeting the man from CBS, but in my youthful ignorance, I decided the company was too small and the salary too low. The other two companies paid considerably more, so I passed on CBS. Fortunately, a year and a half later, I would be given an opportunity to correct this grave error.

I had to wait until my privileged position at Grey Advertising made me miserable before I took control of my own life. I dreamed of having a job I could do with pleasure, enthusiasm, and pride, but at Grey I felt lost, clueless, and disinterested. At a record label, however, I'd be able to demonstrate what I could accomplish through my sheer love of music.

CHAPTER FOUR

THE GREAT ESCAPE

A few weeks after my business-school interview with Procter & Gamble, they flew me to Cincinnati, took me out to lunch at the wonderful French restaurant La Maisonette, and offered me a job starting at $12,000 a year. This was a very good salary in 1969, and I was excited. After eighteen years of formal education, I no longer had to prove my worth to get to the next level because, in terms of job offers, I had already managed to grab the brass ring. Procter wrote the book on marketing, and a job offer from them was as prestigious as admission to Harvard Business School. After a stint at Procter, you'd be more than welcome at any company in the world.

Back home that night, I related the day's events to my wife, Suky. I described Cincinnati, the great restaurant, the town's college neighborhood, and the cachet that came with a job at P&G. I could see that she was happy I was excited, but she sure didn't buy what I was selling. Instead, there was a moment of silence, after which she looked at me curiously and asked, 'Are you out of your mind?' Really. So that was it for P&G.

An offer from P&G was reserved for the very best of graduate business students (which I most definitely was not), so my classmates considered me a fool for rejecting it. The best of the rest looked like Grey Advertising, a major New York ad agency.

I signed on for $11,500 a year. It was an easy commute from the Upper West Side, where I had secured a penthouse apartment on the roof of a building overlooking the Hudson River at 98th and Riverside for $160 a month. Strangely enough, I was assigned to the Procter & Gamble account group and charged with creating an effective marketing plan for the launch of Gain Detergent ('Gain treats stains like dirt').

A couple of months after I started working at Grey, my friend Jon Sweet scored two seats to see The Who at the Fillmore East and insisted I go with him. He and I shared a passion for music, and we enjoyed introducing one another to new acts. Later on, I would come to know every note on The Who's *Live At Leeds*—a sizzling album—but I didn't know much of their earlier work. That night's show was the American debut of *Tommy*. We smoked a little hash on the sidewalk, which made for a memorable evening. Even from our balcony seats, the sound was clear, the performance was superb, and I was transported. The Who were in their prime, emerging from 'My Generation' into the new era of 'Pinball Wizard' and 'The Acid Queen.' The impact of that night focused my perspective on rock'n'roll, and I began to seriously consider a career in music—not as a producer (I didn't know what a producer did), but as a musician.

If Grey Advertising had been anything like the Sterling Cooper Draper Pryce agency depicted in *Mad Men*, I might have enjoyed it enough to remain there, but life at Grey was nothing like life for Don Draper and his hard-drinking colleagues. I might as well have been working at P&G in Cincinnati. 'Cost per thousand' (the price for an advertiser to reach a thousand viewers) was the agency's guiding principle, and every time I entered my small, windowless office, I'd get a hollow feeling in my stomach. I realized too late that the agency didn't send its copywriters out to grad schools to interview and recruit MBAs; instead, they sent the account executives. I never discovered where they got their copywriters from, but if I belonged in an advertising agency at all, I had chosen the wrong floor. In business school, I had glibly referred to marketing as 'advanced common sense.' Regrettably, it turned out to be something of a science instead, and I was always very bad at science.

I never felt so miscast as I did when I took trips to Cincinnati for meetings with the client. There, at Procter headquarters, I was keenly aware that I was not one of the guys. I was one of the few who didn't care all that much about professional sports ('How about those Bengals?'), and in sharp contrast to Grey—where there were at least a few people who shared my social, cultural, and political views—I was clearly out of my element. P&G people had predictably Midwestern Republican values and followed social behavior that was far outside my comfort zone.

Gain's advertising budget for its launch year was eight million dollars—a huge amount in 1969. I attended a couple of focus groups that year, sitting behind one-way glass while a moderator probed the depths of American housewives' minds with provocative questions about their wash-day habits and attitudes. I also attended some commercial shoots—probably the most enjoyable part of my brief advertising career. On the set, I was gratified to discover that when the pitchman held up a t-shirt for the camera, some rules actually applied. If he compared a shirt washed in Gain to one washed in another detergent, both shirts had to be done in the same on-site washing machine and dryer. A real washing machine and dryer were there on the set! I desperately offered this as proof to my judgmental friends that there really was integrity in advertising.

After a few months of Gain, I was moved to the slightly more intriguing Jif peanut butter account ('Choosy mothers choose Jif'), which was a relief, since it got me away from soap and put me on a product that people actually enjoyed. Even so, I felt so uncomfortable about the job as a whole that I grew increasingly disenchanted and depressed. I found myself waking up in the morning and wanting to stay in bed.

As an entry-level employee in a corporate world, I had a windowless office. All the walls at Grey were a flat off-white; offices were furnished only with company-approved furniture and decorated only with company-approved art. We had one of the first fax machines in the city, and, like the apes around the monolith in *2001*, we marveled at it and yapped excitedly among ourselves as we watched the chief of the Puffs Facial Tissue account receive a call from Procter in Cincinnati. As he placed the receiver on the machine's special cradle, a round drum wrapped in a sheet of waxy paper began to rotate and we gazed in awe as the printed text advanced down the page. The whole process took about two minutes, and none of us could begin to grasp how sound could be transformed into print.

One Saturday, I went into the building and painted two of my office walls a muted blue and the opposite two a pale yellow in an attempt to brighten the vibe in the confined space. The result was subtle, but anything was an improvement on white. Looking back, I realize that I should have asked permission before painting a wall that didn't belong to me.

On Monday morning, the head of the Procter account group passed my office on his way in and stopped abruptly to survey the interior.

'Very nice,' he intoned. 'Very nice indeed,' he repeated, then proceeded to his spacious, bright, generously windowed corner office.

When I arrived at work the following Monday, my office walls were a smooth, flat white. No one said a word to me about this. Nothing in the office was out of place. The art was where it had been when I left for the weekend. It was a pure *Twilight Zone* moment. Whatever doubts I had about leaving the agency vanished at that moment; instead of resentment, I felt a sense of relief. By silently repainting my office the way they did, they forced my hand—and, if I had any backbone at all, I had no choice but to bail.

* * *

It was a good time to make a move. In 1970, the culture was turning the corner—women were burning their bras on the streets of Manhattan, secretaries from Queens were smoking joints outside office buildings on their lunch break, and I was moved by songs like 'Let It Be,' 'Fire And Rain,' and 'Woodstock.'

The only person I trusted at Grey knew that I wanted to get out of there, and he arranged for me to meet Tom Wilson, a friend of his who had produced several Dylan LPs. After our meeting, Tom encouraged me to go ahead with my plan to try to get work in the recording industry.

Hot on the heels of the paint incident, I sat down and wrote a letter to Clive Davis, the president of CBS Records. Fortunately, Clive passed my letter on to Bruce Lundvall—the same man who had interviewed me at the business school. Bruce reached out and suggested that I come in for a chat. Suddenly there was hope.

Bruce set up a few meetings for me at the label. I met with VP of business affairs, Walter Dean, and with the Columbia label's director of A&R, Kip Cohen, who had come to CBS from Bill Graham's Fillmore East organization. Walter said he'd like me to go out with one of the Epic Records A&R men to a concert at a high school in Westchester and offer my critique of the band. He was aware that I was a musician, but how much did I know about talent scouting?

I accompanied this nice Epic fellow, Joe Tocci, and when I returned to my apartment late that night, I wrote a detailed critique of the show—the band's look, their presentation, their equipment, their instruments, their strengths and weaknesses as musicians . . . virtually every aspect of the band but the length of the drummer's hair.

A few days after I submitted my report, Walter called and said he'd like me to meet with Clive Davis. For a young music fan in 1970, a meeting with Clive was like a Catholic seminary student scoring an audience with the Pope.

CHAPTER FOUR | 41

After work one day in October of 1970, I walked across town to meet with Clive. The stately and imposing CBS Building at 52nd and 6th—'Black Rock,' as it's known, and still my favorite building in Manhattan—had gone up five years earlier. If buildings wore clothes, this one would have been dressed in a perfectly tailored three-piece charcoal-gray pin-striped suit. It was bold and elegant, and its appearance spoke of the importance and distinction of the CBS organization and its CEO, William Paley. There were genuine Herman Miller Eames chairs in the waiting areas. This building reeked of success.

Clive's suite of offices was on the eleventh floor. I'd seen a few nice offices, but never an actual *suite* of offices, and I was surprised to find that Clive employed two secretaries who were still hard at work even though it was well past 6pm. When I was ushered into his office, he apologized for my brief wait, explaining that he had been on the phone with Bob Dylan. My head swam. I would come to understand that Clive very much enjoyed his associations with famous people—their talent and importance reflected directly on him. Meanwhile, I was twenty-six and thrilled just to be in the presence of someone who actually knew Bob Dylan personally.

Clive and I chatted for a short time, and I applied what I considered a soft sell, explaining how I was an MBA from Columbia, currently employed by a prestigious company, and an ardent rock fan and musician, well suited for a sophisticated outfit like CBS Records. He said that the people who had interviewed me had good things to say, but there were no openings at the Columbia label. Instead, he offered me a job assisting the director of A&R at Epic Records, the smaller of the two CBS labels.

In an instant, my life was transformed. I felt absolutely giddy, certain that I was finally free from the bondage of a frustrating and unhappy work life.

In 1970, the Epic Records artist roster still included The Dave Clark Five, Bobby Vinton, Donovan, and Sly & The Family Stone—not the most vibrant list. Next to Columbia (Dylan, The Byrds, Simon & Garfunkel, Chicago, Blood Sweat & Tears), Epic was the little brother. But never mind—I was in rock'n'roll now, and my mood had soared from resignation to elation in the space of a few seconds.

I decided to walk home from CBS to Riverside and 98th. As I made my way uptown, I rejoiced at the prospect of being able to tell everyone that I worked in rock'n'roll, instead of sheepishly admitting that I hawked laundry detergent on Madison Avenue.

I submitted my resignation to Grey, where the head of human resources expressed surprise and disappointment at my unhappiness there. When he learned of my new position, he asked if I might like to be the account executive on the RCA Records account. I politely declined. I was starting a new job that I considered as good as a job could ever be—although I had no idea of what I'd be doing, or what 'A&R' stood for.

What I did know is that I could go to work dressed in jeans, boots, a t-shirt, and a denim jacket, and let my hair grow—and, at the age of twenty-five, the notion of having a position of responsibility in a major corporation in Manhattan and showing up to work dressed like a freak was delightful.

At Grey, I'd been working for people I didn't respect, doing something I didn't enjoy or know much about, but at Epic I'd feel confident about my instincts. I was off on a journey I had been dreaming about for years.

SIDE B
THE EPIC YEARS

CHAPTER FIVE

THE BEST JOB IN THE WORLD

Beyond my joy and increased feeling of self-worth, joining CBS gave me a sense of pride, since the company was regarded by most as the best in the business. The Columbia label had a diversified artist roster that was the envy of the industry. Other labels like Atlantic and Warner Bros had important artists too—Warner Bros was an LA-based label run by very creative free-thinkers, Atlantic was the creation of a more urbane group of jazz and blues fans, and their respective rosters reflected this difference—but Columbia had household names like Bob Dylan, Santana, Chicago, Blood Sweat & Tears, Miles Davis, Barbra Streisand, Simon & Garfunkel, Johnny Cash, The Byrds, and so many others. And that was only in 1970—bigger things were yet to come.

My office was on the thirteenth floor of the imposing Eero Saarinen–designed CBS building. The interior was furnished with tables and chairs designed by Mies van der Rohe, and many of those same pieces of furniture were on display just down the block at the Museum Of Modern Art. During my time at Epic, our annual record sales grew from $12 million to $240 million, but the number of offices and national headquarters staff hardly grew at all. We took up very little space for the powerhouse we had become. The whole New York staff occupied just fifteen offices.

On my first day in the fall of 1970, I arrived early. The offices on our half of the floor were empty except for the one belonging to Don Ellis, who was already at his desk. Don was then the label's director of marketing, and a year later he would become vice president of A&R, making him my boss. He was welcoming and helpful on that first day, and he questioned me pretty extensively about my musical knowledge and taste—a bit like another interview.

Don was proof that there were people in the record business who were sharp and who had a good sense of humor, but who hadn't been 'formally' educated. Out of fifteen Epic executives, I was the only one with a master's degree and one of the relative few who even had a liberal arts degree. Ron Alexenburg, the head of the label and a brilliant record man and CEO, had grown up on the mean streets of Chicago, the son of a butcher.

Ron had a roomy corner office with a big leather couch and floor-to-ceiling windows facing both south and east. The room was crammed with all the latest audiovisual equipment and gadgets, which he actually knew how to use. He had earned his position through his effectiveness as a great promotion man and was nicknamed 'Ronnie Records.' He was a vinyl junkie who didn't necessarily know much about how records were made, but he loved them passionately.

Sandy Linzer was in the office next to mine. When I started at Epic, he and another staff producer, Barry Kornfeld, were the only other A&R men at the label. Sandy was primarily a songwriter who had written some big hits for Frankie Vallie and The Four Seasons, including 'Let's Hang On,' but as talented as he was, neither he nor Barry was in touch with this 'hard rock music' thing that was developing in the early 1970s.

I soon learned that all other departments regarded the A&R department as the flashpoint—the buck started here, and the promise of a label's success depended largely on the quality and taste of its A&R staff.

Don walked me to my office, and I was delighted to find that it had a floor-to-ceiling window overlooking 52nd Street. Every office in the building had moveable walls, so the size and shape of each one could be changed easily. This office was twice the size of my office at Grey

Advertising, and it was equipped with a powerful amplifier, turntable, cassette deck, and professional TEAC reel-to-reel tape deck. It also had an upright piano—a holdover from the 50s, when songwriters would sit down at the piano and play you a song they were plugging for one of your artists. The piano tuner would come to the CBS building every couple of months—for him it must have been like painting a bridge. There were probably twenty people working for Epic and Columbia who had pianos in their offices.

I was in heaven. A kid on Christmas morning. A pig in shit. I thought of my friends coming from their law-firm cubicles and closet-sized interior offices to visit me in my new office with its floor-to-ceiling window, stereo system, and, of all things, a piano!

The company had decorating guidelines for offices and supplied the artwork for your walls. Personally selected artwork was discouraged—except on the creative floors, like ours. The 70s were so relaxed that for a time I had a large framed poster on my office wall that read 'Enjoy Cocaine' in perfect Coca-Cola lettering.

Over the first few weeks of work at Epic, I developed a routine. I'd take the 7th Avenue IRT subway down from 96th Street, get a bagel with cream cheese and a coffee across the street from the building, and begin my work day before nine. I would happily have started earlier, but no one else was on the floor that early. If I didn't have a lunch meeting somewhere in the vicinity (55th Street between Sixth and Fifth was loaded with good restaurants), I'd usually get a cheeseburger or a hot dog and some well-done fries from Burger Heaven at Fifth and 52nd and eat lunch at my desk. Had I not had a wonderful wife and children at home, I would have been content to live in my office.

Until the explosion of rock'n'roll in the 60s, Epic had been primarily a jazz and classical label. My third-grade introduction to classical music, the *Peer Gynt Suite* by Edvard Grieg, was on the Epic label.

CHAPTER FIVE | 47

The New York Epic Records staff occupied half of the 13th floor. There was a satellite office of about six people in LA and a network of local radio promotion men around the country who reported to the regional heads of promotion. In New York, there were four A&R men, along with the heads of promotion, marketing, artist development, sales, and accounting. Each of the product managers had responsibility for a small group of artists on the roster and would serve as a liaison between the Epic label and the CBS Records art department, advertising, copywriters, and business affairs people who were downstairs on another floor, and who served all the labels—Columbia, Epic, and our 'custom' or associated labels. These smaller, custom imprints would make distribution deals with larger labels like us, since we had the worldwide marketing and distribution networks all in place. We distributed the likes of Monument Records (Roy Orbison) and Philadelphia International (The O'Jays, Harold Melvin & The Blue Notes). These labels had their own creative people and delivered finished records to us. We would create the art and handle the distribution, marketing, promotion, and publicity.

My first boss was Larry Cohn, a major fan of the blues and a wonderful guy who played guitar and had great disdain for corporate structure. He loathed it, in fact, and made no effort to hide his feelings. Larry delighted in not attending boring staff meetings and ignoring forms and reports. He was something of a music purist. He was a sweet guy who treated me like a son but delighted in biting the hand that fed him.

CBS Records was easily the most corporate of all record companies, so Larry did not routinely curry favor with Clive, who fired him not too long after I arrived... but not before Larry, in a fit of generosity and revenge, walked me over to Manny's Music in midtown Manhattan, the premier music store in the city, and treated me (on his CBS credit card) to a Guild D-55 acoustic guitar that cost $400—a fair amount in those days. I still have it, and it was used on some of the records I produced. Bret Michaels strummed it on 'Every Rose Has Its Thorn,' making it a valuable instrument. Larry was a warm and good man, but in his flowered Western shirt, jeans, and cowboy boots, he was just not cut out for corporate life.

My job description was intentionally vague. In brief, they gave me a company American Express Card and told me to go find the next big thing. I had an expense account that was generous enough, and, unlike many of my seasoned colleagues, I was good about not abusing it. CBS Records was very profitable at the time—and getting more profitable each year—so most department heads and senior VPs tended to spend money like water. And, since those VPs were the ones who approved our spending, they were usually forgiving when we filed our expense reports.

This permissiveness applied especially to business lunches and dinners. All you needed to do was provide the name of someone in the industry and the alleged purpose of the meeting, and there were no questions asked—even if you never said a word at the meal about the record business. In the beginning I was very careful, and I reported expenses to the penny. When I filled out my first expense report, my secretary, Barbara, laughed and told me to just round things up to the nearest dollar, or I'd ruin it for everyone else.

Department heads and bigwigs at the label expensed record albums and cassettes, limos, expensive dinners, televisions, stereo equipment, newspapers, magazines, personal car mileage, tickets to any club or show or movie, messenger service, home phone bills, and anything else that might be vaguely categorized as a business expense.

My expense allowance had to be increased when I started traveling more to see bands. I'd usually skip the outrageously priced breakfast at hotels, grab a donut and a coffee down the block, and bring it back to my room. As a result, I was called down to the accounting floor, where a bean counter asked why I was reporting cash expenses instead of using my Amex card. I replied that I was saving the company money by not having breakfast in the hotel restaurant—or, even worse, in my room.

The accountant told me to use the American Express card—even if the expense was greater. They preferred a greater expense accompanied by an official record rather than a cash-register receipt. When the accountant's questioning became too aggressive for comfort, I told him that he had some balls, grilling me about my nickel-and-dime expense reports when I was trying to save the company money while spending days and nights hundreds of miles away from my family on Epic's behalf. I never heard from the accounting department again.

In the office, I received unsolicited tapes—reel-to-reel and cassettes—from managers, lawyers, publishers, booking agents, songwriters, and independent record producers. After a few weeks, I found I was able to evaluate a demo pretty accurately by listening to half of the first song, a minute of the second song, and just the first few seconds of the third song, and I'd know if it was worth listening any further. I stuck with this formula for years, and fortunately I never passed on any act that became successful (Meatloaf excepted). When I listened, I'd busy myself with paperwork or phone calls, or look out of the window; if the music was good enough to distract me from what I was doing, I'd go back and give it a closer listen.

After I began to feel comfortable at the label and more familiar with my colleagues, I enjoyed working at Epic so much that I eagerly looked forward to Monday morning. On Sunday mornings, Don would have the A&R staff over to his apartment on the Upper East Side, where we'd review an advance copy of *Billboard* magazine and its pop singles and album charts, and discuss records we were planning to release. There were bagels, lox, cream cheese, coffee, juice, pastries—a delicious spread. It was something we all enjoyed and looked forward to. In the office, our work day was totally unstructured, except for the regularly scheduled staff meetings, which were critical in terms of informing each department of all the other departments' activities and plans for every release.

There was a relaxed and light vibe on our floor. There were about twenty-two of us, including the secretarial staff, and everyone truly enjoyed being there; there were few complaints, lots of camaraderie, and lots of laughing. Still, there was serious work to be done—sales, accounting, artist development, promotion—and we were always aware that our jobs depended on the success we created. But we were not men and women at work, we were men and women at play. Our product was not consumer goods, insurance, or anything industrial; it was music, and music was art. The head of national promotion would be on the phone all day, and when a local promotion man somewhere in the country succeeded in getting a record added to one of his local stations' playlists, the promotion head would ring a bell on his desk, and we'd all stop by his office to see which record was added to what station. I couldn't imagine a more pleasant office environment.

The weekly 'singles meeting' was not a gathering for unmarried employees, but rather a meeting of representatives from each department, designed to allow us to select and schedule our single releases most effectively. It was held on Tuesdays in a large conference room at the longest and widest conference table I'd ever seen.

Epic head Ron Alexenburg would chair the meeting, and Clive Davis would sit directly to his right. An engineer in the adjoining control room would play a single on cue, and we'd all listen, and then discuss plans for the timing and support for its release. Frequently, Clive would make comments on the song. He wanted people to consider him a renaissance man—not just an attorney or a famous label head, but a brilliant talent scout and savvy music man, which in many ways he was.

During a playback, he'd occasionally stop the music and make a suggestion about the mix of the record—for example, 'The vocal needs to come up in the third verse.' Several people would dutifully scribble a reminder to make sure the vocal came up in the third verse, even if the release was just a week away. Meanwhile, the record's producer, who had mixed the record in the first place, was most likely busy working on another project somewhere far away. Most of us knew that raising the level of the voice in the third verse would require returning to the same studio where the song was originally mixed, securing the same engineer to mix it, setting up the mix just as it was originally set up, and, finally, raising the level of the vocal in the third verse, as requested. Then the record would have to be remastered. This could take a couple of weeks.

Clive, though brilliant, didn't seem to be bothered by pesky details like this, and it wasn't prudent for anyone to point these things out to him in the company of two dozen other record industry professionals. Still, he was extremely talented in a great number of areas, and his resilience and continued success have made him a living legend. I saw little of him during his time at CBS Records, but each time I ran into him later in my career he greeted me warmly, and by name. This meant a lot to me.

The last time I saw Clive was at the Broadway show *The Band's Visit* in January of 2018.

'Hello, Clive, you hired me in 1970 and changed my life,' I reminded him. 'I just wanted to say hello and thank you once again.'

He appeared to be delighted by this. 'Of course I remember you, Tom,' he replied.

* * *

It wasn't unusual for someone to stop unannounced in my Epic office and sit down to talk for a while—not about anything specific or even work-related. If you were good at what you did, no one cared how many hours you spent on the thirteenth floor. The freedom was heady.

On some days, a few of us gathered after lunch in one product manager's office and had dessert, which consisted of a few lines of cocaine on his desk, just to provide a little zing for the afternoon's tasks. Sometimes I'd leave the floor for a while and visit a friend downstairs at Columbia, or maybe in the publicity or business-affairs department. I just told my secretary where I was going, and she'd cover for me. I spent a good amount of time chatting with one fellow who became my personal attorney after leaving the company for a private firm.

Although secretaries weren't yet called 'assistants,' that's what they were—underpaid right hands. The corporation had pay ranges for all positions, and most secretaries were only modestly compensated because the demand for their jobs was high. Given the choice between an accounting firm and a hot record company, young urban women far preferred to be in an environment that offered them free albums, a relaxed workplace, complimentary tickets to clubs and concerts, and the opportunity to meet rock stars without having to deal with the humility of the backstage scene.

Some of the secretaries dated some of the artists, since in those days there was no company policy limiting an employee's activities outside the office, and certainly no 'Me Too' movement. One morning, a secretary who had dated Bobby Vinton the previous night told us about her evening. They had drinks and dinner at a romantic French restaurant; she was excited about the possibilities the evening presented, and didn't know quite what to expect when he took her back to his apartment; there, to her disappointment, they spent the balance of the evening listening to Bobby Vinton records. Another secretary developed a serious long-term relationship with Richie Furay of Poco, one of our favorite and more successful bands.

Once in a while, the corporate guidelines would prove to be counterproductive; after one of my secretaries left to pursue a musical education, I was approached by May Pang, who was looking for a job. May was John Lennon's paramour; in a highly unusual move, she had been asked by Yoko to accompany John on an extended trip to the West Coast, as a kind of assigned mistress.

May was a wonderful person, and naturally I was thrilled at the prospect of spending even a little time in John Lennon's company, which would have been exciting and would have provided access to all sorts of musicians, but the personnel office (they weren't yet 'human resources') wouldn't allow me to hire May because she failed her typing test. She was just too slow for corporate guidelines. Once again I felt I wasn't important enough to argue the case, but I certainly should have.

There were always cartons of tapes on my office floor, and occasionally I'd come in on a Saturday morning to wade through the material so I could catch up. I took this job seriously because I knew that the musicians took their music seriously. There was constant pressure on A&R to deliver the goods, and there were hundreds of guys who were more than ready to take my place if I didn't come up with a hit. Everyone in every other department regarded A&R as the glamor position, and they all would have jumped at the chance to be part of it.

While most A&R men sent form letters of rejection, I wrote a personal letter with every tape I passed on, trying to explain to the artist why his or her music wasn't good enough, or wasn't 'the kind of thing we were looking for.' I took special care when I wrote to musicians who had sent me tapes from prison—and there were quite a few. I knew about Charles Manson and his hounding of Terry Melcher, who had produced some of my favorite recordings from the 60s.

The managers, agents, and attorneys who were shopping artists usually wanted to sit with me while I listened to their tapes. I was uncomfortable with this, and after a few months on the job, I decided I wouldn't do it any longer. I'd thank them for the submission and tell them it wasn't fair to them or to the artist if I listened in conditions that were less than ideal for me. I said I'd listen at home when I was relaxed and focused. Most of them understood.

At night, I'd go to clubs to hear bands that I'd been told about or that I'd heard on tape. If I told the artist's representative that I thought the tape was good enough to merit a live hearing, they might arrange a showcase. I might also decide on my own to fly out to see a band perform live, regardless of how far it took me. Flying was exciting and enjoyable back then, and during my tenure at CBS, I visited almost every state in the country and flew so frequently that I'm in the American Airlines three-million-mile club, and 'executive platinum' for life.

The band's manager would make arrangements for my local transportation and lodging. I'd travel in anything from the manager's own car to a limo and stay at anything from a Holiday Inn to a five-star hotel. To the bands, I was 'the guy from New York'—the label representative with the power to change their lives completely by making them rock stars. I could fly into a town like Fargo, North Dakota, in the dead of winter, where I might hear an act that I loved, and to them, I was the guy who could deliver them from their drab and dreary life to one of wealth, comfort, and debauchery. Consequently, whenever I flew in to see a band, I was treated very well and offered a variety of sins. Had it not been for my family, my responsibilities as a husband and father, and what little discretion I could muster, I might have perished in a sea of wretched excess.

* * *

CHAPTER FIVE

As a CBS Records A&R man, I achieved a certain street credibility. After a year or so, club bouncers and doormen came to recognize me, and I could skip the lines outside many of the popular clubs in Manhattan. I was a regular at the Bottom Line, Trax, and JP's on the Upper East Side (where Billy Joel was the house 'piano man'), and I frequented CBGB's, Max's Kansas City, the Bitter End, the Village Vanguard, the upscale Reno Sweeney, and many others.

One evening in the early 80s, when I was in New York to master a finished album, a few friends and I went to a new club, the Limelight, down at 20th Street. It was a very trendy club in what had once been a beautiful little church, and it was a brand new scene to a relatively old guy like me (a record guy in his forties). I'll never forget walking into the only bathroom, which was no longer a men's or women's room, and seeing the row of stalls—some with a pair of men's feet, some with a pair of women's feet, some with both, some with two pairs of men's feet, some with two pairs of women's feet, one with two pairs of women's and one man's—and women checking their makeup at the sink while men stood at urinals only feet away. There I was, a record producer from famously decadent Hollywood, yet shocked at what I was witnessing in a nightclub. Things change.

One night, I was backstage at a *Saturday Night Live* show when Paul Simon was hosting, and after the show I was invited to the after-party for cast and crew. At this time, the *SNL* after-party was just about the hottest ticket in town, and I found myself seated at a small dinner table with Gilda Radner and her assistant. Years later, after her marriage to *SNL* guitarist G.E. Smith, we were both at a show at Trax on West 72nd Street. I stopped by her table and said, 'Hi, Gilda—I know you don't remember me,' and she chirped, 'Of course I remember you— you're Tommy Werman!' Nothing in my life ever went straight to my head so quickly.

On another evening, after a group of us went to see an Epic act perform downtown, we were offered a lift in a limo back to midtown, courtesy of our well-connected CBS publicist, Susan Blond. She wanted to take us all to Studio 54, and, having never been before, I was excited to see the interior of Sin Central. We were dropped off just outside the entrance, where a group of about fifty hopefuls clustered on the sidewalk behind the velvet rope, beseeching the doorman to make their dreams come true by considering them cool enough to go inside. I took one look at this scene, thanked Susan for her efforts, apologized, and told her there was no way I'd subject myself to that kind of humiliation. While Susan may very well have been privileged enough to waltz right in with us, I never did get to see the interior of the fabled Studio 54.

Later on, after Epic moved me to Los Angeles, I attended a company party at the house of Don Arden, Ozzy's manager. Don lived in a big house way above Sunset Boulevard. It was there that I met Sharon, Don's daughter, who eventually became Ozzy's wife. Though I spent little time with Ozzy—who tended to talk more than listen—I was impressed with Sharon.

A few days later, there was a company staff meeting in the conference room just off the Carlsberg Building lobby. All the departments delivered reports, bringing everyone up to date on their activities. The associated labels were included in this meeting too; their artists would occasionally drop by and sit in or just make a brief promotional appearance, and on this particular day Ozzy and Sharon were invited to the meeting by Epic's West Coast publicity director. Curiously, Ozzy was holding a few white doves as he came into the meeting room. He released a couple, took a seat on the knee of a female Epic staffer, and then, without warning, bit one of the doves' heads clean off.

There are many different versions of this story, but this particular version indicates that the response was one of unanimous revulsion and disgust. Ozzy was asked by Larry Douglas, the chairman of the meeting, to leave the room. Naturally, the director of publicity, who had most likely orchestrated the whole thing, fed it to the press—and thus was born the infamous tale of Ozzy biting the head off a bat. Ozzy reportedly did bite an actual dead bat's head off at one of his concerts after said bat was thrown onto the stage by a fan in the crowd. I was also told by Vince Neil that once, while Ozzy was on tour with Mötley Crüe, Vince bet Ozzy that he wouldn't snort a line of ants on the sidewalk. Vince lost the bet. So, if you've heard some stories about rock musicians and these stories sound ridiculous or unbelievable, don't be too quick to dismiss them.

* * *

Each summer, CBS Records held an enormous convention in a big city hotel somewhere in the world for several days. After attending meetings and workshops all day, the company would gather in the main ballroom at a lavish dinner show for up to twelve-hundred label employees, managers, agents, attorneys, and rock stars. After dinner, some of the label's biggest or newest artists would perform for the crowd, which was peppered with celebrities and musicians from around the world.

Clive invited many special guests to these shows, and the CBS artists who appeared benefited greatly from the experience. A strong live performance at a convention was as valuable as a comedian's successful debut appearance on *Johnny Carson*—it would establish an act firmly in the minds of the company as one who deserved to be well promoted and marketed, and a great show could launch an artist's career. At Columbia and Epic in the 70s and 80s, if the company liked and believed in the artist, every employee would make that act's success his or her personal responsibility. This kind of commitment was both admirable and unusual for a record label.

CHAPTER SIX

EVERYONE WANTS TO BE AN A&R MAN

In the 70s and 80s, the A&R man (apologies—there were very few A&R women at the time) was primarily a talent scout. The quest to find a hit act was exciting, but it came with constant pressure—a musical version of *publish or perish*.

A&R is short for 'artist and repertoire,' and originally the A&R man's job was to find the right song for the artists assigned to him. If you were Sinatra's A&R man, the most important part of your job description would be to find the next 'Come Fly With Me' or 'New York, New York.' You met with music publishers, agents, attorneys, and songwriters; they'd come to your office and play an assortment of tunes—on the turntable, the tape recorder, or the piano—that they thought might be appropriate for Frank or another one of your artists.

Over the years, the job description evolved. With the emergence in the 60s of the singer/songwriter and bands who wrote their own material, the A&R man was no longer just a liaison between the publisher and the artist, but also a talent scout who sought out great acts that might also be writing great songs. There were still songwriters, and there were still artists who recorded songs written by other people, but by the 70s, the A&R man was primarily concerned with finding a self-contained hit act that did both. He'd discover performers, bring them to the label, and oversee the making of their albums.

While I felt capable of distinguishing the promising from the poor, I discovered that it took me three or four exposures to a song before I was confident enough to express an opinion.

CHAPTER SIX | 59

Veteran manager Cliff Burnstein surprised me in my office one day and asked me to listen to the newest single by his band Def Leppard. He handed me a cassette of 'Photograph,' which he was obviously excited about. As we listened together, he smiled and anticipated my enthusiasm. I reacted enthusiastically because I liked and respected Cliff—he was a good guy and an important manager with a great ear—and I didn't want to disappoint him. But while I thought it was very well produced (as is all of Mutt Lange's work), after one hearing I didn't really love the song.

After I'd heard 'Photograph' on the radio several times, I did come to like it, but it took me a few plays to get there. When it was released as a single, it went to #12 on the *Billboard* Hot 100, and in 2009 VH1 named it the thirteenth best hard rock song of all time.

My inability to instantly identify a hit concerned me, so it became my practice to spend a little more time than the average A&R man would before I confidently made up my mind about a song. Rarely would the demo version of a song sound good enough to justify my seeing the act in a live performance. In New York or LA, this could mean attending a showcase or a club performance.

Showcases were like private auditions held in rehearsal halls, usually in the late afternoon, so that label people could conveniently evaluate an act without having to sacrifice an entire evening. They were far preferable to the club scene. It was more comfortable, there was no waiting, and there might be food and drink. If I was told the band would play at nine o'clock, I was there at ten minutes to nine. In a club, the band might be an hour and a half late, but I never dared to risk missing a potential hit act just because they might have been punctual on the very night I decided to arrive late at the club. If I added up all the time I spent sitting, eating, smoking, drinking, gazing at my watch, and waiting for a band to go on, it would total several months.

In a quarter century of going to clubs, not one act I saw ever hit the stage on time—not one. In some cases, they could be up to two hours late. Club audiences became so used to this occurrence that they would routinely accept the delay and continue to spend way too much money on expensive, watered-down drinks.

In LA, small clubs would frequently agree to book a new unproven band, but only if the band agreed to bring a minimum number of friends with them—friends who had to pay the cover charge and buy a minimum number of drinks. This policy was known as 'pay to play.'

If a club was presenting a new band with a small following—or no following at all—they might deliberately delay the band for quite a while, and the audience—mostly friends or relatives of the band—sat and drank because they had no other choice. Even so, many new acts preferred to have label reps see them in a live club setting, where their friends and family provided a very appreciative audience, rather than at a showcase in the sterile confines of a rehearsal studio, with no applause at all.

One night, Guns N' Roses were scheduled to do a set in the ballroom of an old hotel in downtown LA at 11pm. This was unusually late for me, but I'd never seen the whole band perform live, and I'd been given a couple of tickets by my friends at Geffen Records. At 1:30 in the morning, I finally gave up waiting for the band to show. I never did find out if or when they appeared, and I never did see them play, other than briefly, and without Axl, in a tiny rehearsal room off the Sunset Strip. More on that later.

If I heard a good band from another state, I'd find out when they could do a live show, schedule a couple of days out of town, and make travel plans. In that case, the band would make an effort to be punctual, since they knew I'd made the effort to fly out from New York for the sole purpose of seeing them.

CBS had an in-house travel department to arrange our trips, and they tried to make traveling as painless as possible. After I became an established staff producer at Epic Records, my contract stipulated that a town car would pick me up at home and take me to the airport, where a representative of the travel agency would meet me and take me to the airline's VIP lounge. I'd fly first class and be met at the other end by another town car, which would take me to a nice hotel. I'd put all meals and other business expenses on the CBS American Express card. These luxuries made traveling for work not only easy, but downright enjoyable.

Even in my first year at the label, my lifestyle on the road was considerably more comfortable than the one I could afford at home. In those days, when people were buying records like food and record companies were making money hand over fist, labels could afford to treat their employees generously. In 1980, I flew with my Epic colleague Larry Hamby from LA to Sydney to see a band and to meet with AC/DC's management team about a new act they were shopping. The first-class round-trip airfare for the two of us was ten thousand dollars.

If a band was good enough, I'd meet with them after the show, get to know them a little, and the next day I'd contact their manager, attorney, or booking agent, depending on who had introduced me to the band's music in the first place. Then, for my first few years at Epic, the next step was to involve my boss, who would need to see them as well. Later in my career, I was able to sign acts on my own.

Many weeks could pass between first hearing the band and a signed contract. During that time, other labels could become interested too, and the small ones could move far more quickly than a big corporate label like CBS, Warner Bros, or Atlantic. If an act was good, and if the word on the street was that a record label was taking a close look, A&R interest in that act could explode.

The A&R community behaved like lemmings—no one wanted to be caught napping when there were potential hit acts to be snatched. Once a band started to attract attention, things moved very quickly. Usually, there was about a month of intense hype around an act, during which time A&R people would swarm, keeping a wary eye on other labels' reps and agonizing about whether or not to take the leap, sign the band, and put their careers on the line. If a month or more passed and the band was still unsigned, interest would tend to dissipate; with each passing day, the band's chances of being picked up became fewer and fewer. If no one had bitten after a couple of months of industry interest, that act was usually history.

* * *

Later on, after I became an established producer, going to clubs in LA came to be something of a problem. Unsigned musicians would troll the room with demo cassettes in their pockets, and I was both flattered and dismayed when they recognized me, introduced themselves, and handed me their demos. It was a little like a Bar Mitzvah or an Italian wedding, where friends and relatives discreetly hand you an envelope that you slipped into the inside pocket of your suit jacket. I grew to be more and more guarded about meeting new people, since they didn't really want to know me but simply wanted something from me. In LA, this was done more obviously and more frequently, and I was grateful for the safe haven of the studio, where no one could get to me. I was a soft touch when it came to accepting demos—I felt it was rude not to do so. But not one unsolicited tape I was ever handed outside of the office turned out to be worth even a second listen.

I was a pretty conventional A&R man, in both behavior and appearance. Over the years I learned that in the entertainment world, the stranger your appearance or behavior is, the more fascinating you're considered to be, and the more respected your professional ability is.

Two good examples are Roy Thomas Baker and John David Kalodner. For starters, both of them used their middle names, which was unusual, except among Richard Nixon's close circle of associates. But in the record business, this practice just served to strengthen one's identity.

Roy was a flamboyant and zany Englishman, always making fun, cracking jokes, smiling and laughing, driving a Rolls, and speaking at a very fast pace, but never appearing to concentrate, focus, or labor over anything at all. This made his achievements in the recording studio seem fairly effortless—and Roy's achievements were anything but modest. Producing Queen was enough to make him a star, and his quirky personality and presentation just added to the picture.

John David Kalodner was an exceptional A&R man whom I first met when he was at Atlantic Records in New York. At the time, the record industry was building its West Coast presence, and John eventually moved on to Geffen Records in LA, where he would sign, guide, and resuscitate many successful acts. Rather than relying on tact, John bluntly spoke his mind about almost everything. He saw people as either geniuses or jerks. He pulled no punches and expressed his admiration or disdain without hesitation. For John, hardly anything fell between really great and totally worthless, and he communicated this freely. He also had a very long beard, which was unusual in those days—especially for a record guy—and you could frequently find him in a white linen suit, like the one favored by John Lennon.

A&R was the department of choice at any record label. The creative function was the most interesting, the most glamorous, and (in time) you could earn a bundle if you could deliver the hits. By the 90s, A&R men would receive a small percentage of an act's record sales, and you could become a millionaire from one big record. While I was well compensated for the albums I produced, I always wondered how much more I would have earned if I had been paid this kind of modest royalty from the start on the more than 125 million albums sold by the bands I had signed to Epic Records.

Music is, of course, subjective. Listeners are inspired by all different kinds of music, and one person can respond positively to a song while another might not be able to tolerate it. But in the A&R world, there are certain standards of quality. What I sought was a band whose music was unique and something that both I and the record-buying public would love.

CHAPTER SEVEN

THE A&R MAN SCORES... AND THE ONES THAT GOT AWAY

Just a few weeks after I started at Epic, label head Ron Alexenburg gave me a test pressing of a finished album he wanted me to evaluate. An independent producer named Paul Leka (composer of 'Na Na Hey Hey Kiss Him Goodbye') had produced the record in his home studio in Connecticut and was now shopping it to labels. The album was strong, with two standout cuts, 'Sophisticated Lady' and '157 Riverside Avenue.' The band's unusual name was REO Speedwagon.

I wrote a positive evaluation and sent it to Ron as a formal office memo. I'd been schooled in the proper style of business correspondence by Procter & Gamble, who insisted that all memos from their various advertising agencies follow the same format and were required to start with 'This is to...'. I recommended that we look into this band further. He returned my memo with a handwritten note:

Go right ahead, my good man.

So, after only a few weeks at Epic, I was taking my first official business trip.

I was met at the airport in Champaign, Illinois, by a young recent graduate of the University Of Illinois. He was serious—all business, not much time for pleasantries. You could tell right away that he was bright, that he didn't suffer fools, that he knew exactly what he wanted, and that he seemed to be on a mission from God. Later, as we walked from the motel to his office, he told me his plans for the two artists he managed—REO Speedwagon and an unknown singer/songwriter from the area named Dan Fogelberg. What he laid out for me was so ambitious that I thought it was laughable.

Who does this guy think he is, I thought to myself, *Superman?*

This was Irving Azoff, and in his show business career he would accomplish just about all there was for anyone with a show business career to accomplish. Later on, in Los Angeles, he was generally considered to be the only man in town who could go up against David Geffen and win. He also had a reputation for doing whatever it took to achieve victory.

Irving's partner in those days was John Baruck, who became a friend of mine and later organized a big annual music business golf tournament at the wonderful Pebble Beach Golf Resort—the Kelly–Baruck Invitational. On the first night, there was a barbecue buffet dinner. At this dinner, the 'new guys' traditionally stood up and said a few words about themselves and how they came to be invited. When Irving took up golf and began attending this annual event, he convinced Glenn Frey from the Eagles (whom Irving managed) to come up with him and play in the tournament.

At this barbecue on the first night, Glenn got up and introduced himself.

'Hi, I'm Glenn Frey, and I'm in the Eagles. I don't know most of you, but we all have something in common: we've all been lied to by Irving.' Hoots and big applause. But Irving was fiercely dedicated to his artists, and his artists were loyal to him; REO was just the beginning, but considering his lifetime of achievements, one could certainly regard him as Superman.

When I saw REO for the first time back in 1970, they performed at the Red Lion, a large club in Champaign that was popular with university students. They were a powerful band with a big, full sound.

The lead guitar player played fast, deftly, and barefooted; the keyboard player was excellent; the drummer was tasteful and solid; the bass player kept everything anchored; and the singer was dynamic. They did an excellent cover version of 'Sympathy For The Devil'—not an easy thing to do.

After the show, Irving hosted a party at his apartment for about forty people who had been at the club. It was one of the more intelligent and interesting groups of people I've encountered at any rock'n'roll gathering—avid music fans, but also current or former students of the university.

REO Speedwagon went on to sell over forty million albums. Signing them was a significant thing for me, but it did little to provide me with any credibility as a talent scout, since my attempts to bring my next three discoveries to Epic were rejected by the label's new head of A&R after he replaced Larry Cohn.

*　*　*

An A&R man can make two big mistakes: he can turn down an act that becomes successful, or he can sign an act that never amounts to anything. Any A&R man who spends more than a year or two in his position will almost certainly make the second error at least once—he'll sign an act he believes in, but for one reason or another the act will be a stiff. The fault won't always be his; record labels can drop the ball in a number of ways.

When it's all said and done, though, the A&R man had his chance at bat, but he swung and missed. In the 70s, an A&R man's batting average needed to be at least .200 for him to survive. Some A&R men will sign one act that becomes huge and then never find another one. If that act is big enough, though, he can ride its coattails for years. The same holds true for a producer; some producers might have had a hit with only one act but are given plum projects for many years afterward, based on that one big record.

REO Speedwagon was my first signing, and the band has been a consistent moneymaker for Epic Records since 1970. They've been on the road for over fifty years now. Fortunately for me, my next three signings—Ted Nugent, Cheap Trick, and Molly Hatchet—developed into big hit acts as well. But in the five long years between signing REO and signing Nugent, I found three acts that I was dying to bring to the label—all three of which were, unfortunately, rejected by Don Ellis, who had replaced Cohn.

Epic could have had these acts for a pittance, too, because there wasn't a shred of interest from any other label. Regrettably, Don didn't find them attractive enough, and at that time in my young career, I lacked the confidence to argue my case. I could have been persistent; I could have tried to convince him to trust me, and that each of the bands was going to be huge, but at the time I simply didn't have the nerve to risk signing what might have turned out to be a loser.

It's one thing to love an act and have others love it too, but it's entirely different when your colleagues don't share your enthusiasm. You're out there on a limb. You need everyone in your corner. For a record to be a hit, every department at the label—promotion, sales, publicity, artist development, marketing—needs to be enthusiastic about your act, because you depend on them to deliver the goods.

If they don't like an act that you think is great, it makes you pause. It makes you bite your cuticles. After a band's killer show, when the lights come on in the club, you look around the room and ask yourself, *Where are the other labels? Why am I the only one who likes this band? Why aren't there any other A&R people here? Why isn't there a bidding war?* This uncertainty can erode your confidence and make you doubt your own musical taste.

The fact that my immediate superior dismissed these three bands made it worse. I was happy working for him; he was a great guy and a great administrator. He was older and wiser, and he had previously been the manager of a large Record Store in Madison, Wisconsin. There, he befriended musicians like Boz Scaggs, Ben Sidran, and Steve Miller, developing a refined taste for a type of music that was clearly not as visceral as the music I favored. He knew enough about pop, but not enough about the kind of aggressive rock'n'roll that was beginning to appeal in a big way to me and to millions of young record buyers.

I enthusiastically presented him with three bands I had found in the space of two years, but while I was very excited about each of them, he was dismissive, and his opinion alone was enough to keep me from risking his respect for my taste. I liked him a lot—he used sarcasm endearingly, and had a great sense of humor—so it was tough for me to deal with his rejections. I desperately wanted to convince him that he was mistaken. If I'd had the confidence and courage to do so, I might have had the kind of giant success that earned the occasional A&R man his very own record label...

* * *

In 1971, I was approached by Ron Johnsen, an engineer who had completed most of an album for a band called Wicked Lester. He did the project at Electric Lady, Jimi Hendrix's studio on 8th Street, down in the West Village. The power-pop he played me in my office was worth another listen, and I was curious about Hendrix's studio anyway, so I decided to sit in on a couple of sessions. After a few long evenings in Electric Lady's control room, I recommended that Epic purchase this nearly completed album.

It was a modestly priced 'master purchase,' meaning that the label liked the way the album was developing and agreed to finance the remainder of the recording. This was a commercial-sounding pop album with lots of layered backing vocals, harmonies, and plenty of hooks. The two driving forces in the band were Stan Eisen and Gene Klein, a couple of nice Jewish boys from Queens. Six months later, they would adopt the stage names of Paul Stanley and Gene Simmons.

Epic did purchase the Wicked Lester album, but the band broke up before we could release it. Since album releases were almost always supported by a live tour and we had no band to put on the road, the LP was relegated to the vault, where it would sit untouched for several years. Meanwhile, Paul and Gene had formed a power trio—Gene on bass, Paul on guitar, and a drummer named Peter. They phoned to ask me if I'd come to see them perform a set in a rehearsal room near Union Square in Manhattan.

Anxious to salvage our modest investment in Wicked Lester, I agreed to come along and bring my boss with me. Arriving at the rehearsal room, we found the three band members dressed in black Spandex, their faces covered in white greasepaint. Gene and Paul were in boots that laced up to just below the knee, on top of what appeared to be six-inch heels. This put Gene at about six-foot-four—an imposing figure indeed. At the end of their set, he picked up a galvanized bucket of what we thought was water and tossed the contents at us. We ducked, but it turned out to be shiny silver confetti.

I was delighted—the songs weren't brilliant, but they were catchy enough. Most importantly, the choruses were memorable enough to sing in the shower. The element of fascination, though, was the theatrical aspect—my first exposure to an early example of rock music as performance art. The band's presentation was colorful, imaginative, and entertaining, and each of them had his own comic-book superhero persona—and of course there was Gene's tongue.

We thanked them and walked back downstairs to 23rd Street, where

Don stopped, turned to me, and said, 'What the fuck was that?'

My heart sank. I couldn't respond. I felt awkward and uncomfortable, so I didn't argue. He didn't get it, and I was bummed.

About a year later, Casablanca Records signed KISS, and Neil Bogart, the label's founder, wisely purchased the Wicked Lester LP from Epic for about $60,000—and buried it. If we had released that album in an effort to take advantage of Gene and Paul's eventual fame, the lightweight pop music would have reflected poorly on KISS, when compared to the hard rock that they had become known for—and with which they would go on to sell more than one hundred million albums worldwide.

* * *

A few months later, I received a cassette from a Canadian manager named Ray Danniels. The music on it was almost avant-garde—not your average earthy rock'n'roll. It was intelligent rock, memorable and catchy; the songs' arrangements were as complex as those of Yes, and their musical style would come to be known as 'progressive.'

I flew to Toronto, where Ray picked me up and took me to dinner before we drove out to a high-school auditorium in the Toronto suburb of Mississauga. The band was a power trio—drums, bass, guitar—and they were superb. I was impressed by their musicianship and the ease with which they played. This was highbrow rock'n'roll; it offered something different, and *difference* was a quality that every A&R man sought.

I went backstage right after the show to tell the band I'd love to sign them to Epic Records. I returned to my Holiday Inn that night feeling triumphant, excited, and hopeful—I'd finally be able to demonstrate my good taste by signing a musically legitimate, commercial 'art' band.

Back in New York the next day, I typed up a memo to Ron Alexenburg. Fortunately, there was no objection to the music this time, but the CBS business-affairs department, which had the responsibility of negotiating the deal with the band's attorney, flatly informed my boss, Don, that the money for this deal was 'way out of line.' The band's attorney was asking for a $75,000 advance for two albums. Imagine that. But CBS was a publicly held corporation, and certain financial guidelines had to be honored. Although $75,000 is small change for today's record labels, back then it exceeded those guidelines, so there was no need for further discussion.

Once again, I'd been let down by my label. A few months later, Cliff Burnstein, then a young A&R man at Mercury Records, signed the band—and Rush, as they were known, went on to sell more than twenty-five million albums and earn over twenty gold records.

* * *

At the time, of course, neither the label nor I could grasp how enormous my boss's errors in judgment were, as it would take a few years for these two bands to really take off. But as if this wasn't sufficient punishment, the same thing happened again!

In 1972, a softly spoken, well-dressed gentleman named Alan Walden came to see me in my office and, in his quiet, engaging, and rather syrupy Southern drawl, told me about the rock'n'roll band from Georgia that he managed. Unlike most of the casually clad managers who came calling, Alan was dressed for the city, and his presentation was so laid-back and articulate that I found myself leaning forward and listening closely, trying not to miss a word. No jive, no bullshit—just a quiet manner and a convincing, honest enthusiasm for his band.

Alan and his brother Phil had founded Capricorn Records, home of The Allman Brothers. His presentation was effective, and so was the music. He left me with a reel-to-reel tape of eight songs that I had transferred to a CD years later, after the band's demise, which still sits on a shelf in my office. I think the reel of tape itself is somewhere in the attic.

At that point in time, I had never heard a band with a three-guitar attack and those signature Southern riffs. This was a unique style—a kind of blues rock, but sweeter, and with more harmonies. It was a 'chorus line' of guitars, all in sync, all playing the same complex line in three-part harmony. It definitely rocked.

I flew to Atlanta, rented a car, and drove through a hard rainstorm to Macon, Georgia, where I saw Alan's band, Lynyrd Skynyrd, tear up a rural roadhouse with their driving Southern rock songs. I'd never seen a band with two drummers before, and I loved it. They would set up on opposite sides of the little stage, playing different patterns that somehow worked perfectly together. The smoky club couldn't have held more than a hundred people, but for a weekday night, it was jammed—everyone was totally into it. Bobbing heads, stomping feet, free-flowing alcohol, fists in the air, wild dancing...

Once again, I returned to New York and did my best to convince the boss that he must see this band. He agreed to do so, and a few days later we flew to Nashville together to see them play at a club called the Exit In. Once again, the band tore it up, and the audience went wild.

As we walked through the parking lot after the show, Don turned to me and said, 'Good band—no songs.' Despite the fact that 'Free Bird' had been in the set. And that's how Lynyrd Skynyrd rounded out the trio of big fish that had wriggled away from my musical net. Some months later, fellow producer and keyboard player Al Kooper saw the band and signed them to a production deal. The band sold thirty million records. Collectively, KISS, Rush, and Skynyrd ultimately sold a total of over 150 million records.

* * *

By now, it was 1975, and my initial feeling of frustration had become one of disgust. I was disheartened, depressed, and unsure I had a future in the music business. I'd gone against my parents' wishes when I left Grey Advertising, and I dreaded having to admit to them that they were right when they said I was throwing my life away by going into rock'n'roll.

I contacted my cousin, whose family owned a few upscale restaurants in Manhattan, because I was beginning to think about going into the food business. I had been at CBS Records for five years, but aside from REO, I hadn't done anything I could hang my hat on. I was struggling to get by on a meager salary that had begun at $10,000 a year and had gradually crawled up to $18,000—barely enough to keep pace with the cost of living.

There I was at a small rock record label, having been formally trained to compete in the far more hazardous cut-throat corporate arena—and it seemed I was being thwarted at every turn. My MBA was designed to prepare me for a position as CEO, but my lifelong devotion to music had given me an ear for hits. I needed to find a way to prove my worth, and I was feeling enormous pressure to make this happen. I did love the work, so I did my best to hang in there.

In my career as an A&R man, I never passed on a band that became a hit, but there were a couple I didn't sign who went on to achieve a fair level of success. One night, Alan Walden took me to a club in Tampa to see The Outlaws. I liked them well enough, but I'd already signed Molly Hatchet, and the two were too similar. On another evening, I went to the Mercer Arts Center in New York to see Manhattan Transfer, a wonderful swing vocal group that I'd seen first at Reno Sweeney, a cool little Manhattan supper club. I didn't think Epic would understand their music that well, or know how to market them, so instead of trying to sign them, I wrote a memo to all the members of the Columbia

Records A&R staff, urging them to see this act. Columbia's roster had the artistic variety and breadth necessary to successfully deal with a niche act like this. I got no responses, and a few weeks later Manhattan Transfer was signed to Atlantic Records.

I also went downtown to see The New York Dolls at the Mercer Arts Center, with both Clive Davis and Atlantic Records president Ahmet Ertegun in attendance. It wasn't unusual for several different labels to be at the same showcase, but to have the two most important men in the East Coast music industry at the same showcase was unusual—and probably a little awkward for them. They sat in different rows and didn't speak. Clive got up to leave after three songs, and Ahmet followed a couple of minutes later. He didn't leave simply because Clive did; they just weren't enchanted with the Dolls, who were eventually signed to Mercury Records.

In the mid-70s, the Annual CBS Records Sales Convention was held at the Grosvenor House in London. On the first morning, I walked along Park Lane with my friend and Epic colleague Gregg Geller, on our way to a marketing presentation down the road at the London Hilton. As we left this meeting to return to the Grosvenor House for lunch, we encountered a young man on the sidewalk, singing a song and playing an electric guitar through a small amplifier strapped to his back. There was a little sandwich board on the pavement reading, 'Stiff Records welcomes CBS Records to London.'

Gregg and I stopped to listen. About a minute into the second song, I told Gregg I was returning to our hotel for lunch. The music didn't captivate me. Gregg said he wanted to hear some more, and he wound up signing the singer to the Columbia label. And that's how Elvis Costello came to be a Columbia Records artist. Apparently, Elvis was arrested for being a public nuisance shortly after I left for lunch. I never did acquaint myself properly with his music. You know the saying about 'one man's meat...'

So yes, I did pass on a few bands who became well known, but I didn't miss out on any 'monsters.' Many A&R men do. Some poor guy passed on The Beatles just before they were signed to EMI, and The Who actually included one of the pass letters they received in the sleeve of their *Live At Leeds* album. I sympathized with the unfortunate A&R man who had written that letter.

The label rep who argued with Queen about releasing 'Bohemian Rhapsody' as a single was certainly roasted nicely in the movie of the same name. Apparently, these A&R men didn't hear what many of us later considered to be something undeniably great, but I think it was pretty cold to rub their noses in it. After all, until Boston's manager came to us at Epic, a whole day's worth of appointments had failed to move even one other New York A&R man. As they say, there's no accounting for taste.

CHAPTER EIGHT

ABRACA-DABRA, I'M TED NUGENT'S PRODUCER

What injustice could 'Terrible Ted' Nugent have suffered that would eventually put him politically somewhere to the right of Attila The Hun? Back in the 70s, Ted (then probably what one would call a 'committed conservative') and I (a liberal Democrat) were able to find common ground on two political issues: gun ownership and the death penalty. We honestly never discussed politics any further than that.

Almost fifty years later, it remains a challenge for me to explain to our 'progressive' friends my professional and personal friendship with a man who's become one of the most radical and outspoken voices of the right. So I'll try again.

The fact is that Ted is a good guy. He's smart, articulate, sincere, capable, and honest. You would want him in your foxhole. The Ted I knew was a well-prepared, well-equipped outdoorsman and the happiest, most carefree rocker of them all. I prefer to recall the Ted of the 70s, and I need to separate that personal Ted from today's very outspoken political Ted. I find many people on the far right as personally objectionable as they are politically objectionable, but you'll just have to take my word that Ted was—and probably still is—a pleasure to hang out with. That Ted Nugent—the one I recall—was also a major figure in the trajectory of my career.

In 1975, following Epic's rejections of KISS, Rush, and Lynyrd Skynyrd, I wasn't exactly feeling professionally secure. I was worried about my lack of achievement at the label. A year earlier, before I met Nugent, I had walked into my boss's office to return a tape, and as I placed it on his desk, I spied a handwritten note to him from Clive Davis.

I don't think Werman has developed a singles ear yet.

I didn't know what had prompted this note, but I was shattered. After work that afternoon, for the first time since the day I was hired, I walked the fifty blocks uptown home to my apartment.

About six uncomfortable months later, a fellow named Lew Futterman came to my office and announced with no little enthusiasm that 'Ted Nugent & The Amboy Dukes' were no more, and that Ted Nugent was now available as a solo act. I tried to show a little interest; beyond The Amboy Dukes' one charting single, 'Journey To The Center Of The Mind,' I knew absolutely nothing about Nugent. What I found curious was that a group of hard-rocking Midwestern teenagers had chosen to name their band after a book written by Irving Shulman about a fictitious Jewish street gang from Brooklyn.

Ted was signed directly to Lew Futterman's production company, which meant that Lew could serve as either manager or producer, or both. The contract gave Lew control over the most critical areas of Ted's career.

Coincidentally, the Epic A&R department was scheduled to visit Chicago to attend a concert by the label's new band, Labelle—another one signed by my good friend and colleague Gregg Geller. Since it was important for A&R and marketing personnel to be familiar with all of the label's music, about ten Epic folks were making the trip to Chicago.

Lew arranged to have Ted do a show for me at the nearby Illinois Institute Of Technology the night before the Labelle concert. That evening, there couldn't have been more than a few hundred people in the audience, but Ted exploded onto the stage with a Tom Cruise 'Risky Business' slide, grabbed the microphone, shouted 'Hiya I-I-I-I-I Teeeee!' and continued at absolute maximum output for the next hour.

I had never before seen this much energy or intensity from an unsigned performer. The band was strong, the rhythm guitarist/singer was great, and the songs were simple, driving, and memorable—each written around a distinctive guitar riff, like that well-known riff in 'Cat Scratch Fever.' Onstage, Ted was confident, outspoken, tall, thin, wild-looking, and very amusing—definitely long on charisma.

I was pumped. This guy was my cup of tea—hard rock with pop hooks. I was in. I felt the same excitement of discovery that I had experienced when I first heard KISS, Skynyrd, and Rush, and once again I was the only A&R man in sight. This time I had no second thoughts, no doubts. If I wanted to sign him, he was mine to sign. I was determined to see it through, make my stand, and convince any doubters that we should sign this guy, no matter what resistance I might encounter. I knew right away that Ted could make hit records, and he and his band would be a home run on the road, supporting and promoting the album.

I went backstage and expressed my enthusiasm, trying to maintain a measure of professional cool. We had a great meeting. I liked this guy.

Back at the hotel, I called my new boss, Steve Popovich, and convinced him to accompany me to Ted's next gig. Better still, David Krebs, a successful New York manager who did a lot of work with CBS, heard about my enthusiasm for Ted and offered to put him in the opening slot for Aerosmith's tour stop at the Ice Arena in Lansing, Michigan. This was very good for us—Aerosmith were breaking big, and opening for them would expose Ted to hundreds of thousands of Aerosmith fans—his target demographic.

We arrived early at the arena and stood near the door, watching the audience troop in. It was a packed house. Almost every fan—boy or girl—was clad in head-to-toe denim and motorcycle boots and had shaggy long hair. It was an army of disenfranchised metalheads, all looking to blow their brains out on Friday night. Even though these kids were there to see Aerosmith, the native Michigander Ted Nugent drove them crazy.

Following that show, Lew Futterman made a deal for Krebs to manage Ted. Within a year, Ted would be headlining the Academy Of Music in New York and hosting Andy Warhol and Truman Capote backstage, the two legends stopping in for a photo opportunity with the Motor City Madman before continuing uptown to Studio 54.

On the flight back to New York from Michigan, I found myself seated near Ina Meibach, a well-known music-business attorney who represented The Who. I told her how excited I was about Ted, and suggested that he and Pete Townshend might make a good pairing in the studio—that maybe Pete would consider producing Ted's debut album for us. Ina was amused. She delicately implied that Pete was out of Ted's league. To her great credit, when Ted's debut album went gold, she sent me a nice personal letter of congratulations.

Before we recorded that album, I flew out to spend a day with Ted at his farm in Hanover, Michigan—a small community about an hour outside of Detroit. I drove along a country road, passing home after modest home as I looked for the right mailbox number, seeing clothesline after clothesline with sheets, towels, underwear, and denim overalls blowing in the wind, until I came to one with Spandex tights and fringed shirts. This must be Ted's place.

Ted loved guns as much as he loved guitars, and he showed me his collections of both before we went out into the field to do some target shooting. I hadn't held a weapon since summer camp when I was ten and we had target practice with .22-caliber rifles.

Afterward, we sat in the living room, where Ted explained his musical philosophy. He made liberal use of the term *gonzo*, accompanied by a tightly clenched fist. He described the kind of album he wanted to make and exactly how he wanted to approach it. The intensity with which he laid out his recording plans made it clear to me that not only did he know exactly what he wanted, but he also hadn't come close to achieving it yet. Ted was known for his aggressive lyrics, but it sounded to me as though he wanted his music to be threatening, as well.

For dinner, he barbecued a wild boar he had killed with his bow and arrow. It was delicious, and I had seconds. It occurred to me that had I been a vegetarian, Ted may not have wanted me involved with his music at all—the wilderness was so important to him. For years afterward, he sent us venison and bear steaks for Christmas. I never did develop a taste for them, but we very much appreciated the thought.

Ted and I did not discuss politics. Among rock musicians in the '70s, there was little or no discussion of such things in the studio, or even over dinner. The conversation usually centered around sex, drugs, and (especially) rock'n'roll. In defense of my continued friendship with Ted Nugent, I continue to emphasize his character and let people know that he has integrity and is a straight shooter—pun intended. I try to explain his perspective on hunting; his belief that the only difference between his way of securing food and 'our' way is that he kills his own meat rather than having a factory farm or slaughterhouse do it for him. He uses the pelts for clothing and rugs. He's a supporter of Ducks Unlimited, a nonprofit dedicated to the conservation of wetlands and other waterfowl habitats. He understands the need for 'thinning the herd' when the number of deer or other creatures becomes too great for the land. He believes it's more humane to kill animals than to have them suffer a slow death from starvation.

Ted would bring along a life-size dummy deer to the studio and practice his bow-hunting technique between takes. The rest of us could barely draw the bow back. He would express his frustration with groups like PETA, who give him a very hard time about his hunting. Personally, I think they should be directing their criticism at trophy hunters like Donald Trump Junior, who prefers to hide behind bushes with a big rifle and slaughter defenseless animals so he can put their heads up on his living room wall.

Ted grew up with guns. He's always been licensed to carry, and he's always carried. One day, I met him for lunch at Jerry's Deli near my home in Studio City, California. He arrived before me and was waiting inside when the place was held up. He recounted how he had pulled his weapon and pursued the robbers into the parking lot, but he couldn't get a clear shot.

One night after we had finished recording Ted's first album, I was in a limo with him and his booking agents on the way to his show at Detroit's Cobo Hall. As the car neared the hall, one of the agents told us to lock the doors. When we exited the limo and headed for the stage door, I saw that both agents and Ted were carrying shoulder-holstered guns. During the show, I had to duck behind the PA stacks at the sides of the stage to avoid being hit by flying cherry bombs. At the end of the show, some fans in the balcony lit their seats on fire. Not unusual for a Motor City rock'n'roll show in the 70s.

Ted has always been incredibly energetic and optimistic. The world is his oyster, and he can't see any reason why he doesn't deserve to have exactly what he wants; he does understand, though, that he has to earn it. He's always expressed how much he loves his life, and if you spend any time with him, you can see he's not kidding.

Offstage, Ted was very much the same as when he was performing—outspoken, irreverent, quick-witted, and fast-talking. He sucked up all the energy in the room when he walked in. He defined the term 'cocky.' Being more of a conventional type myself, I enjoyed all of this immensely.

I wanted to help Ted get his attitude down on vinyl. But there was a problem. In my enthusiasm to sign Ted, I hadn't realized that Lew Futterman expected to produce the record. This concerned me because, as much as I liked Lew, I didn't have the greatest regard for his rock'n'roll aesthetic. I decided that I had to spend as much time as I could with him in the recording studio, in order to protect my investment and my reputation. It was five years since I had signed REO Speedwagon, so the success of this new project was critical for me.

For this recording, my role was really to be the label's representative in the studio, responsible largely for quality control. If Ted's Epic Records debut was a stiff, I couldn't imagine holding onto my job any longer.

Fortunately, the recording process turned out to be pretty straightforward. Lew had made a cost-effective deal with a studio in Atlanta called the Sound Pit, so named because the recording room was a short flight of stairs down from the control room. The Sound Pit was located in the heart of downtown Atlanta and was allegedly owned by a convicted murderer. I stayed at the brand-new Omni Hotel complex just a mile or so away. I'd fly into Atlanta on Monday morning and fly back to New York on Friday evening.

The sessions were punctual and productive. Ted ran a tight ship. It took us less than a month to make the record at a bargain cost of about $25,000.

During my first visit with Ted in Michigan, he had made it clear that he had the album all worked out, and he proved this in the studio—particularly with what became the album's first song and a Ted Nugent classic, 'Stranglehold':

> *Here I come again now, baby*
> *Like a dog in heat.*
> *Tell it's me by the clamor now, baby*
> *I like to tear up the street.*

People just didn't write songs like this in the 70s. It would be a decade until hip-hop artists were writing lyrics that proclaimed, 'I'm badass and you're not.' Not only did Ted have that attitude, but he had written a song that expressed it—with all the parts arranged, note by note.

Lew mixed the entire album after I had returned to New York, but the results were disappointing. I rejected the mix and asked my boss for an extra $5,000 so that I could do my own. He agreed, and I returned to Atlanta and went to work with engineer Tony Reale with one goal in mind: getting Ted's aggressive attitude on vinyl. (Tony was a fine engineer who would also record my first solo production, Cheap Trick's *In Color*.)

I did the best I could with just three pieces of outboard gear—echo chamber, tape slap, and phaser. I created guitar duets from Ted's single guitar lines, threw in a lot of echo and repeats, recorded backward stereo cymbals, and created a few other tricks.

I was happy with the result, and, to his credit, Lew agreed that the remix was better than the original. We sent it to Ted, who called to say the album was great and that he particularly liked what I had done with 'Stranglehold.'

'But don't ever do anything like that again without asking me first,' he added.

I was contrite, but delighted that Ted was happy with the finished product. Lew and Ted were generous enough to give me an album credit as co-producer. *Abracadabra*—I had suddenly achieved my dream of being a record producer. A few months later, I learned that

Epic's release of the album *Ted Nugent*—produced by Lew Futterman and Tom Werman—had sold over a million copies.

* * *

Over the next four years, I produced four more albums with Lew and Ted. Ted and I understood each other creatively. We knew how rock'n'roll should make you feel—it should energize you and it should be edgy. I think Lew understood that we had this musical perspective in common, and with each project, he restricted himself more and more to the recording of just the vocals. Ted and I dealt with the music, and Lew made it all possible: he oversaw Ted's separation from The Amboy Dukes, secured a record deal for him, and got him a first-class manager in David Krebs.

Lew was well compensated for his troubles, getting about twenty-five cents a record to the five cents that Epic gave me as a performance bonus. At the time, I was okay with that.

I enjoyed spending time with Ted. His humor was ever-present and could show up unpredictably. I remember hanging out with the band in their backstage trailer before an outdoor show at a Midwest fairground when Ted called me over.

'Hey, Werm, want some popcorn?' he asked, cradling a big cardboard popcorn tub in his lap.

I reached in and almost took a handful of his erect penis, which he had inserted through a hole in the bottom of the tub. I recoiled in horror, and he fell out of his chair in hysterics.

After a session in Atlanta one night, we went over to Alex Cooley's Electric Ballroom, the premier musical venue in town. We were shown right up to the VIP section, where Ted spied Ronnie Van Zant slumped over a table, totally wasted, with his head in his arms.

'Watch this,' he said to me. He bounded over to Ronnie, put his hands on his shoulders, and started shaking him violently, jabbering in his ear.

'Hey ya, Ronnie, how ya doin'? What's up, man? What's shakin'? How ya feelin'?'

This amused everyone around him, and most of all Ted himself. He had a lifelong disdain for anyone who drank or used drugs.

Girls—he liked. Following one coliseum show back at the hotel one night, I called Ted's room. He told me to come up and said he would leave the door ajar. I walked into his room to find him in bed, leaning back on a pile of pillows, both arms around two very cute young blonde girls. A glass of warm milk sat on the night table. I figured he had set this scene for my benefit and wonderment. The next morning, I asked him about the girls and he said he would only keep company with 'clean' young girls; in this particular case, he assured me that he had obtained their parents' permission for a weekend visit. His strategy, he explained, was to ask the parents if they'd rather see their daughters out with him or out with irresponsible high-school guys who drank and used drugs. This frequently did the trick.

While I got along well with Ted, I also enjoyed hanging out with the band's other guitarist and main vocalist, Derek St. Holmes, an energetic and funny guy who, like the rest of the band (and me), enjoyed drinking and smoking weed. Derek proved his talent on the first album by writing and singing 'Hey Baby,' which earned the band's first significant airplay.

Unfortunately, Derek would occasionally go over the top. He liked to goad Lew, whom he considered a 'suit.' He got himself arrested one night during the Atlanta sessions for the second album, *Free-For-All*, and this was the last straw for Lew, who wanted to teach Derek a lesson. He barred Derek from the studio and began searching for another singer to finish the vocals.

I knew only one great vocalist who was free at the time—Meatloaf. Lew had never heard of Meatloaf (who hadn't yet been signed to a label), but he was desperate to find an instant replacement for Derek. Meat agreed, and he was in the studio the next day. He sang four songs on the record and is even credited on the album cover, but I don't think many of Ted's album buyers ever noticed.

Meat's voice wasn't at all appropriate for a Ted Nugent album, but he was delighted to have the opportunity, and he didn't hold back. The result was a metal opera. I missed having Derek in the studio, though. Despite his occasional irresponsibility, he was a great singer, a great guitar player, and a very entertaining guy.

In support of those first two albums, Ted opened for some pretty big acts, including Aerosmith, Black Sabbath, KISS, and Lynyrd Skynyrd, and I enjoyed the freedom of watching these shows from just offstage, thanks to my laminated 'All Access' pass. When Ted opened a sold-out show for Sabbath at Madison Square Garden, the Ringling Brothers circus animals were all backstage. Regrettably, there were also some animals seated in the audience. A few minutes before the show, I spied a guy standing just behind a barricade near the stage, holding up a bedsheet with a racially offensive message in black magic marker. Shocked and furious, I hurried over to him, as if to conceal someone's embarrassing nakedness, and reached over the barricade; I grabbed him by his t-shirt and yanked him toward me.

'Put it away or I'll break your neck,' I yelled in a rage.

Maybe it was the laminated pass, maybe it was my clenched teeth; either way, it worked. Adrenaline can enable you to do some extraordinary things. Some of Ted's fans weren't particularly well-behaved and embraced sociopolitical viewpoints that were definitely contrary to mine. Sometimes it was uncomfortable; sometimes it was terrifying.

While we were in Miami finishing *Weekend Warriors*, my fifth and final record with Ted, I got a call from my boss asking me to fly to Tokyo, where Epic would be recording Cheap Trick's live show at Budokan. They were very big in Japan, and I desperately wanted to go, but I couldn't just walk out on Ted. By remaining in Miami for one more week, I missed the opportunity to produce Cheap Trick's enormously successful *Live At Budokan*. Meanwhile, *Weekend Warriors* turned out to be my least favorite of the five albums Ted and I did together, and in fact it was my last record with him. I recall telling my boss that I felt Ted's material wasn't changing enough from record to record, and that I wasn't excited at the prospect of doing *Rocky 8*.

Forty-seven years after we met, Ted's still on the road; he still fills concert halls with rabid, devoted fans, some young, some more old. He still hunts, and while some folks mellow with age, Ted's opinions seem to have hardened to the point of petrification. But he has more integrity than just about any other rock star I've worked with, and he's the only one who still gives me credit—and gratitude—for understanding and safeguarding the character of his music.

CHAPTER NINE

BOSTON: THE A&R MAN STEPS IN SHIT

A&R people like to recite a list of the successful acts they've signed, just as they like to avoid mentioning the ones they turned down who went on to be hugely successful at some other label. I thought I was pretty good at seeking out and finding musical talent, and to sign or to pass was a perilous decision to make. Once in a great while, though, an A&R man would get lucky and a hit act would simply knock on his door and jump right into his lap.

Lennie Petze was a former Epic Boston promotion man who had risen to regional head of promotion. He asked me if I thought there was a place for him in our A&R department in New York. I liked Lennie a lot, and eventually he came to New York to join the A&R staff. Late one afternoon in the fall of 1975, Lennie walked into my office with Paul Ahern, a friend of Lennie's and a fellow Bostonian. Paul was in New York for the day to try to get a deal for a new band he was managing at the time.

Lennie wanted to get my opinion on a few songs from the band's demo tape. Our boss, Steve Popovich, was out of town, so the three of us went into Steve's office to play the tape, since he had the best sound system on the floor. I put the cassette in and pressed *play*.

The first song, 'More Than A Feeling,' was simply the best demo track I'd ever heard in my life. It sounded like a finished recording. I reserved judgment, waiting to see if the next song was anywhere near as good. It was. By the time we had heard a few seconds of a third remarkable song, I stopped the tape. Looking at the two of them, I asked, 'Is this *Candid Camera?*'

I was stunned. I couldn't believe this band was unsigned. And Paul had come to his friend Lennie, asking that we sign them. No audition. No showcase. No late-night club gig. We didn't even have to leave the building.

Boston's demo wasn't just rock'n'roll: it was a new, powerful, and very engaging sound—original enough for FM radio, yet at the same time undeniably very commercial. The main component of Boston's sonic appeal was Tom Scholz's signature guitar sound, which was both heavily distorted and heavily compressed, so that it presented as 'polite' heavy metal. This particular sound was made possible by a little invention of Tom's that he had cleverly named 'The Rockman.'

Lennie and I expressed our enthusiasm to Paul, not playing coy, not trying to hide our excitement. It would have been difficult for me to do so when I was so plainly overwhelmed. We listened to a few more songs, and I was giddy. I turned to Paul and said, 'If this band can even come close to reproducing these songs live, we can personally guarantee you a very good deal with Epic Records.'

Of course, I had no authority to say this, but I was certain that anyone with functioning ears would absolutely flip for this music. Both Lennie and I were positive that we had received a present of a big winner here.

I picked up the phone to call the boss.

'Steve,' I said, 'I think we may have just found the best hard rock band in the country.'

Ahern was gratified. He told us that every label he'd seen in New York that day had passed on the band. To this day, I find it hard to believe that any major label A&R man with working ears wasn't stumbling over himself trying to sign this band. Thankfully and miraculously, none of them had bitten, and Lenny and I were grateful to them all.

Two weeks later, he and I returned to see our families in Boston for the long Thanksgiving weekend. On that Saturday, we drove out to Aerosmith's rehearsal facility in a nearby suburb to meet the members of Boston, who played a brief set for us. Scholz had hastily put together a band that could reproduce the music he had recorded by himself in his home studio. While their live presentation didn't quite live up to the brilliance of the demo, it was strong enough. Leading the way was Scholz's churning, heavily distorted/compressed guitar sound that was somehow contained enough so as not to overwhelm the rest of the band.

Scholz, who wrote the songs and played most or all of the instruments on the demo, was clearly the leader and driving force behind the band, but each of the members—particularly Brad Delp on vocals—was more than competent. Sometime later, we found out that Scholz held a master's degree from MIT and had worked as a design engineer at Polaroid. No surprise. He had created the demo in his home studio, playing several (if not all) of the instruments and using the Rockman to achieve his unique guitar sound.

While I wanted very much to be Boston's producer, I had too little studio experience at the time, so Epic recruited John Boylan, a veteran producer who had recently joined our A&R staff; he had produced Linda Ronstadt and had been in her early backing band, the nucleus of which evolved into the Eagles. Thanks to Scholz's genius and John's creative involvement, quality control, and supervision, Boston's first album for Epic went on to sell more than twenty million copies—at that time, it was the biggest debut album of any band in history.

John and I would end up as the two staff producers at Epic from 1976 to 1982. I never asked him about the details of his contract to produce Boston, but as a staff producer, if he had agreed to even as little as a nickel per record as a royalty rate, he would have made over a million dollars on Boston's first album. Had he been an independent producer hired off the street by the label for that one project, he would have earned roughly six million dollars.

In the summer of 1976, CBS Records held its annual convention at the Century Plaza Hotel in Los Angeles. After one night's lavish banquet in the ballroom, I went upstairs to one of the many after-parties and was handed a finished cassette of the just-completed Boston album. I stepped outside onto a balcony high above LA, put my earphones on, and listened to the whole album on my Sony 'Professional' Walkman. I'll never forget that experience, one of the most satisfying musical moments of my young professional life.

CHAPTER TEN

LONDON CALLING

As the Epic A&R man in charge of our small British artist roster in the 70s (including The Hollies, Jeff Beck, The Dave Clark Five, and original Zombies members Rod Argent and Colin Blunstone), I made a couple of trips to London every year, and I loved being there. At that time, England had bargain prices, the restaurant food was dreadful, Carnaby Street and the Kings Road were where it was all happening, and I could bring home off-the-rack, smartly cut velvet suits for $60 each. The youth culture was as vibrant as anything I'd seen since America in the late 60s.

I cabbed everywhere, fast and cheap. I stayed at the Four Seasons on Park Lane and met with the Epic Records UK people and our British artists. The bands I encountered were usually hospitable, courteous, and attentive, even though I was a relative nobody. I represented their record label in America, and I was consequently of some minor importance to them. On the whole, I found these British artists to be less egocentric, more inquisitive, better educated, and more courteous than their American counterparts.

On one of these trips, I brought over an edit I had created in my office for a single release from Jeff Beck's *Blow by Blow* album, produced by George Martin. I was asked to come up with an edit that Sir George would approve, and I decided to take it to his office personally, just in case I could manage to get an audience with the man who in my estimation might have been the greatest record producer alive. I was delighted to find that he had set aside some time for the meeting; he offered me a seat and a cup of tea and asked me quite a few questions about myself—not exactly what I expected from a superstar producer. He was relaxed, courteous, and, of course, well-spoken. I played him the edit, and to my delight, he liked it very much. He suggested we go directly over to his AIR Studios and duplicate the edit on a copy of the master tape so that the single could be released without delay.

It was a rare sunny day, so we walked. There I was, walking down a London street with world-famous Beatles producer George Martin, who approved my edit, took me to his recording studio, and gave me a personal tour. I was pretty jazzed about this, and I'll always treasure the fact that I got to spend most of an afternoon with the man.

On that same trip, I went to Abbey Road Studios to check in with The Hollies. They were recording in a room that was separate from the one The Beatles used, but one of the studio staff members showed me The Beatles' control room. It was empty, and I visualized a session with Paul and John sitting on either side of George Martin in the control room, perhaps while George was recording some lead guitar in the large studio. I was told that the London Philharmonic used the same studio to record. Unfortunately, I was alone on this visit, so there was no one to take a photo of me walking the Abbey Road crosswalk.

That same week, Jeff Beck picked me up and we drove out to his house in the English countryside, where he introduced me to the game of snooker in his drawing room. It was a big deal for me to be afforded this kind of access. Jeff was a subdued, almost shy fellow—unusual for a major rock star. We walked over to his motor pool, where he showed me the hot rod he was working on—he had several. Jeff's fingernails were usually black with the motor oil he had accumulated under them by working on engines. I met his live-in girlfriend, Celia, who served us tea and a sponge cake, which she said she had made especially for my visit. Would this have happened in the US?

CHAPTER TEN | 95

A few years later, I tried to return the favor by accompanying Jeff and Celia to a table at our gala dinner show at that year's CBS Records convention at the Grosvenor House Hotel in London. There were twelve hundred invited guests and CBS Records personnel, and, because of Jeff's importance, we were seated at a table only a few yards from the stage.

I was feeling pretty cool about this situation when I turned around to survey the ballroom and was stunned to discover that Mick and Keith were sitting just two tables away, and George and Ringo were at the table next to theirs. This was unquestionably the peak of my young musical life, and I was truly dumbstruck. Mick flashed a big smile and called out, 'Hello, Celia!' in a way that left little doubt that he had been romantically linked with her at some point. Jeff didn't look happy about this.

After the meal, I borrowed a camera and snapped a photo of Ringo that still hangs in my home office; fortified by several glasses of wine during dinner, I shamelessly followed George Harrison into the men's room, where I waited awkwardly by the sink until he approached to wash his hands. This was an opportunity I couldn't possibly have passed up since I considered George to be the most important figure in all of music.

I introduced myself, hoping his eyes wouldn't glaze over. Desperate to engage him in conversation, I quickly asked some questions about a few of the songs he wrote, and about some of his guitar licks on *Revolver*, the album I thought marked his emergence as a songwriter. With that, he promptly focused on our chat, and in the middle of the Grosvenor House men's room we had a brief conversation about 'Got To Get You Into My Life,' 'Taxman,' and 'I Want To Tell You.' When it was over, far too soon, I floated back to my seat, knowing that for the rest of my life, I would very likely never meet anyone more important to me. This is still true, although Pete Townshend runs a close second.

* * *

Jeff Beck was a world-famous guitarist with a style all his own; following his years with The Yardbirds, he'd played in a number of groups with stellar artists including Ron Wood, Rod Stewart, Aynsley Dunbar, Jimmy Page, Keith Moon, Nicky Hopkins, and John Paul Jones. In the mid-70s, Jeff partnered with progressive keyboardist Jan Hammer for a tour featuring songs from Jeff's *Wired* and '*Blow By Blow* LPs. The tour involved over a hundred dates, and I was asked to be the executive producer for a number of live recordings to be assembled for an album to be called *Jeff Beck With The Jan Hammer Group Live*. My job was to help select the best songs and live performances, and to oversee the mixing and sequencing of the album.

After sitting in the remote recording truck for a few of the shows, I felt that one night stood out as being particularly good. In August of 1976, the group performed at the Astor Theater in Reading, Pennsylvania, a mid-sized venue that reportedly had once been a porn theater. I felt confident that the bulk of the LP would come from that evening's strong show.

When the tour arrived in New Orleans, we had a day off, and I took Jeff into Allen Toussaint's legendary Sea-Saint Studios, where he and I repaired any audible recorded errors from the Astor Theater show. This was a common practice for 'live' albums; usually you would keep the drum track, but if the engineer was able to isolate the sound of each instrument sufficiently, you could repair the mistakes on (or actually re-record) the bass, guitar, and vocal tracks.

That night, I met Jeff, his manager Ernest Chapman, and Jan for dinner in the hotel dining room. We discussed the album, and when I brought up the subject of mixing the record, I suggested that I could take care of this at the CBS 52nd Street studio, where I was to also mix Ted Nugent's *Double Live Gonzo* LP two years later.

'Either I mix the album or there will be no album,' Jan immediately declared, in a voice and an accent that was identical to Arnold Schwarzenegger's. I was pretty deflated about this, but at the time I had no real credentials as a producer, so there was nothing I could do. If you listen to that album and think the keyboards are too loud in the mix, you'll know why.

CHAPTER ELEVEN

CHEAP TRICK: A TREAT

One day in 1976, I got a call from Jack Douglas, who had just produced Aerosmith's *Rocks*, which at the time I considered the best American rock album I'd heard.

Jack knew of my work with Ted Nugent through David Krebs, who managed both Ted and Aerosmith, and he told me about a band from Rockford, Illinois, called Cheap Trick, whom he said he'd like to produce. I had heard a Cheap Trick demo tape before Jack called me, but I hadn't loved it enough to take the next step; however, I had a high regard for Jack's work, so I thought maybe I should give the band another listen.

I flew out to see them play at a club in a strip mall in Quincy, Illinois. A reliable indicator of any band's strength was the size of their local following, and, in the Rockford area, Cheap Trick really packed them in. That night the crowd was ecstatic, but I left the club in some doubt because I thought their performance was way too loud, and the sound was muddled. Sometimes, when it was too loud in a club, I'd go all the way to the back of the room. I did that on this occasion, and I could hear the music more clearly.

As I had done with Nugent, I asked my boss, Steve, to come back to Illinois with me and see the band for himself. That way, if the band succeeded, I'd get credit for 'discovering' them, but if they were a failure, at least I had Steve's stamp of approval, so we would have shared the blame. Unfortunately, this is the way one comes to think as one learns the defensive plays of the record business.

Fortunately, Steve was enthusiastic about the band. Jack Douglas produced the band's first album at the Record Plant in New York. I visited the studio several times to watch the process. The production was honest and accurate, and it captured the band's unpolished, aggressive live sound, but I didn't hear a song that I felt could be a hit single. Still, *Cheap Trick* was well received by the critics. The band sold a few hundred thousand records, and, with the greater success of their subsequent albums, eventually this first record went gold.

When it came time for the second album, Jack was buried in the studio with Aerosmith, whose behavior at that time may have added some length to the project, so the label asked me if I would produce Cheap Trick in his stead. Columbia had also asked me to produce Eddie Money's debut record, and I was a few weeks from starting that, but my mentor, Bruce Lundvall, was now the company's president, and when I confided in him that I would prefer to do Cheap Trick, he helped me out by 'drafting' me for the project, intercepting and deflecting much of the anger from Eddie's manager, Bill Graham. I was excited about this opportunity and relieved to be protected from Graham's wrath, which was well known. This would be my first solo effort as a producer.

* * *

The three albums I did with Cheap Trick spoiled me for anyone else. I loved those sessions. The studio work was quick and painless; each of these four guys was a master of his instrument, and each had a unique style and a unique sound. They were bright, and they had a sharp and healthy sense of humor. There was a lot of laughing. Working with them was a treat, and I awoke each morning eager to get to the studio because I knew the day would be entertaining and productive. While I liked working on most of the albums I produced later in my career, many of them presented me with obstacles, difficult egos, and problems that I never encountered with Cheap Trick. We recorded *In Color* with ease, and *Rolling Stone* named it 'Album Of The Year.' It quickly went gold and ultimately went platinum, but I honestly feel it should have been far more successful.

The basic tracks for *Heaven Tonight* were recorded at the iconic Sound City studio in Van Nuys in the San Fernando Valley, not that far from the Hollywood hills. At the time, the studio hadn't clocked nearly as many hit albums as it had by the time it closed in 2011. We did a lot of experimenting at the studio, like putting Rick Nielsen's guitar amp in the bathroom with the door open and the microphone out in the hallway, or hoisting a 'shotgun' microphone up to the high ceiling and directing it at Tom Petersson's bass amp way over in the corner of the large main recording room. Most of the other sessions for the three albums I did with Cheap Trick happened at my home away from home, the Record Plant on Third Street between Beverly Hills and Hollywood.

Bun E. Carlos is the finest drummer I had the good fortune to produce. His drumming was as good for what he didn't play as for what he did. You can hear his influence in the drumming of some who came after him—even contemporary drummers, like the Foo Fighters' Taylor Hawkins, especially on the album *In Your Honor*. I've heard some of his trademark fills reproduced on other people's records. When he played, he provided a rock-solid rhythmic drive, but where other drummers wore themselves out, Bun E. never seemed to exert himself or even break a sweat.

We'd be finished with a whole album's basic tracks (drums, bass, rhythm guitar) in just a few days, and as soon as we had reviewed and approved them all, Bun would hang a sign on the front of his snare drum that said, 'Gone Fishing.' He would fly home to Rockford, Illinois, and I wouldn't be surprised if he actually did go fishing. This was Bun E.'s entire contribution—we wouldn't see him for the duration of the project.

Tom Petersson is an excellent musician with a distinct sound unlike any other bass player I've heard. While most bass guitars had four strings, Tom's basses had six or eight or even twelve, and he played all of them with ease. His ability to come up with perfect bass parts for Rick Nielsen's songs was not unlike McCartney's with The Beatles. He used two different kinds of speaker cabinets—a Gallien-Krueger unit to reproduce the very bottom of the frequency spectrum, and a Hiwatt to reproduce the very top. We recorded these separately, then mixed them together according to what each song needed. Together, they produced a big bass sound, rather like John Entwistle's—full on the bottom and biting on the top.

Rick Nielsen was different from other guitarists and writers in a number of ways. His songs were unusual, clever, and memorable, and he wrote the majority of the band's repertoire. His playing was zany and humorous, his stage presence goofy and even a bit self-deprecating. His instruments were unique too—some of his guitars had two or more necks, and he played some unusual fretted instruments, like the mandocello. While we were working together, I went over to Rick's home in Rockford, Illinois, met his family, and saw his incredible guitar collection. I always found him entertaining and bright.

I think I may have been the one who came up with the term 'The Man of 1,000 Voices' for Robin Zander. He has a most remarkable set of pipes, and instead of laboring over vocals as I might with a lesser singer, I would get a brilliant performance from Robin in just a few minutes. He could nail lead vocals on two songs in an hour, then go on to double the melody and put harmonies over the top. With other singers, I typically had to pull several vocal tracks together, using different sections from different performances, but Robin could do three takes of a song, so that I could assemble the best lines onto one track, and in thirty minutes we'd have a brilliant lead vocal. It didn't matter if someone else wrote the song and taught Robin the melody and lyrics; his performance was so confident and unique that once he sang a song, he owned it.

During recording, sometimes I'd turn to the group and ask them what they thought of one of my musical ideas. Rick would usually respond with something like, 'You're the producer,' so I got used to interpreting their songs the way I wanted to. I'd introduce piano, Hammond organ, percussion, maybe vocal harmonies—and so it was with *In Color*. By the time we got to *Dream Police*, Rick was much more involved, writing string arrangements and contributing more production ideas once the body of the song (which he had written) was down.

A couple of decades later, there were several argumentative debates in the press between Rick and me about who was responsible for what. In some of their interviews, the band said they weren't happy with aspects of the production on the three records I produced for them. I responded by asking why, if that was the case, they didn't use someone else over that three-album timespan.

The sometimes acrid back-and-forth resulted in a mutual agreement that neither I nor they would speak negatively about the other. I always regretted this development; I was fond of these guys, and I was proud to have signed and produced them. I still feel that *Heaven Tonight* and *Dream Police* are possibly my best productions, and I regret not being able to communicate with Rick, Tom, or Robin. Bun E. and I have been in touch occasionally by email, and he was the only one who expressed gratitude to me when they were inducted into the Rock And Roll Hall Of Fame.

After the third record we did together, Cheap Trick chose Sir George Martin as producer for their next album, *All Shook Up*. This was not an unusual move for a band (engineer, label executive, and producer Jimmy

Iovine once said, 'After three albums, you should shoot your producer'), and I was a great admirer of Sir George's producing, arranging, and performing skills. Still, *All Shook Up* was only a modest success, and it didn't do as well as any of the three albums I had produced. Being only human, I admittedly gained a bit of satisfaction from this fact.

Of all the bands I either signed and/or produced, they were my favorites, and I did my best work with them. It's a strange and sometimes unfortunate business, but we'll probably never speak to each other again.

CHAPTER TWELVE

SO, WHAT DOES A RECORD PRODUCER ACTUALLY DO?

The ideal producer should abandon his personal preferences in order to help the band realize its musical vision, but I think many good producers don't do this at all. While I was willing to collaborate with a band to make them happy, I usually approached the music to please myself—and hoped the band would be satisfied with the result.

I'd been at Epic for two years when the first Eagles album was released. I loved that record. The songs were great, the musicianship was flawless, and I was impressed by how easy it was for me to hear each instrument. The music and vocals combined to make a beautiful whole, but if you wanted to follow any single voice or instrument, you could. Compared to much of the music of that time, the production was sparse. My attention jumped from one instrument to another. The record was produced by Glyn Johns, who had also produced another of my favorites—The Who's *Who's Next*. I listened raptly to these two albums over and over through a pair of Koss Pro-4A headphones.

Initially, because these two albums were both produced by the same person but were completely different animals, I assumed that a producer was probably the one who organized and funded the project, similar to a movie producer. But Johns had faithfully delivered the sound of each band, even though the two bands were at opposite ends of the pop music spectrum. One was amplified, abandoned, and bombastic, the other refined, measured, meticulous, and partially acoustic...

Back then, I couldn't accurately define the producer's role. I'd bring albums home, put them on the turntable, and flip the jacket over to read the liner notes and album credits. Every album had a 'produced by' credit, but what did this mean? His name (female producers were very few) was listed, but his duties were not.

Even today, when I tell people I was a record producer, most of them think this has something to do with artist management, talent booking, or concert production.

'What did you do before you were an innkeeper?'

'I was a record producer.'

'Oh, which band did you manage?'

* * *

I must have listened to 'Take It Easy' ten times before I heard the banjo. It makes a subtle entrance at the beginning of the guitar solo and gradually increases in volume. By the third verse, it's quite apparent. I've pointed it out to people, but most of them can't hear it well enough to identify it. To make it louder might have interfered with the lead guitar solo, and would probably have given the song more of a bluegrass feel than the band wanted. But it's a great performance by Bernie Leadon, nicely placed in the mix, subordinate to the other fretted instruments but still complementary to them.

Picking out individual instruments in a song, or even in a symphony orchestra, had always been something I found easy, but the older I became, the more I realized that it was something not so many people could do. I began to listen to music in two ways: either I'd hear the whole band's unified performance, or I'd follow one instrument until I was distracted by another one. I could hear if something was too low or too high in the mix, or when too many instruments were occupying the same small frequency range, destroying clarity and making it tough to distinguish one instrument from the other.

It's essential for any record producer—and certainly for any recording engineer—to be able to place each instrument properly in the mix with all the others. Great sounding records are the result of a good producer–engineer team that not only selects the right instrumentation and the best performances but also assigns these performances to specific frequencies and makes sure the final mix occupies as much of the frequency range as it can. This way, each instrument has its own space and is easier for the listener to follow. When you crank the volume, the sound should fill the room and not make you put your hands over your ears.

In the 70s and 80s, it might have taken about two months of twelve-hour days, six days a week, to record and mix an LP. So, during the making of the roughly fifty-two albums I produced, I spent the equivalent of over twenty-five thousand hours in recording studios—that's more than two thousand days, or every single day for six years running.

* * *

For my first few years at Epic Records, I had tended to enter recording studios strictly to visit a session or to edit an album track down to 45rpm single length. CBS owned and operated several full-service studios—two in Manhattan (on East 52nd Street and on 30th Street), one in Nashville, and one in San Francisco.

When I started editing long album cuts down to shorter singles in my office in the 70s, I'd slip the tape into the quarter-inch groove on a metal splicing block and make two little lines with a white grease pencil at either end of the piece of tape I wanted to remove. Then I'd cut the tape on those lines with a single-edged razor blade and reconnect the two ends with an inch of splicing tape. I'd perform this operation in my office, then walk the tape over to the 52nd Street studio.

CBS was a union shop, so only a union engineer was permitted to handle or cut the master tape. To do this, the engineer would retrieve the master from the vault (all tapes recorded at the studio were kept in a locked vault), record a copy, duplicate my splices, and send the result to the pressing plant.

Many producers were unavailable to edit their own album cuts, as they'd be off somewhere else doing their next project, so the label started asking me to edit most of the tunes that were chosen to be released as singles. In the 70s, corporations bought up huge numbers of pop radio stations so they could all be programmed uniformly. Programmers—the people who determined which songs should get radio airplay and how frequently they should be played—became very important in the industry, and radio stations all over the country, owned by the same corporate group and advised by the same independent music programmer, began to sound pretty similar. Even the deejays sounded similar—they offered an exuberant delivery that communicated good cheer and enthusiasm.

Playing fewer discs per hour translated to more ad money per hour, and this was important now that the companies owning the stations were responsible to shareholders. To play more songs and sell more air time, the songs ideally needed to be right around three minutes long.

When I edited down an album cut, I'd try to bring it in at around 2:57, as long as this didn't compromise the song. Almost all of Elvis's early hits are less than three minutes long, and 'All Shook Up' and 'Hard Headed Woman' are actually under two minutes each. Most of them were written to be this length, but as musicians became more self-indulgent or boundlessly creative, editors had to learn to carve the fat from the meat in order to qualify these tunes for an AM station's playlist.

Commercially promising songs usually had long and short versions. A successful album of four- or five-minute songs with lengthy jams might sell three or four hundred thousand copies through FM radio play, but if that same album yielded a big hit single for AM radio, the album might sell two or three million.

My editing experience was useful in preparing me for producing. I'd work with bands whose songs were basically arranged and structured for FM radio, and by restructuring I'd be able to turn one or two of the cuts into an AM hit, hopefully without sacrificing the act's street credibility or musical integrity—and, of course, without anyone being able to hear the splices. I learned to maximize the best parts of a performance and minimize or discard the weaker parts.

Once a few of my edited songs became hit singles, I became the go-to music editor for Epic. Some songs were more challenging than others—the album version of The O'Jays' 'For The Love Of Money' is 7:14, and Argent's 'Hold Your Head Up' is 6:15; my single versions reduced them to 3:42 and 3:15, respectively, requiring many splices in each to qualify them for addition to a Top 40 station's playlist. Through trial and error, I learned how to hear through layers of music—how to listen to each individual instrument, and how to find the perfect spot for a splice. This ability would prove very useful.

* * *

During my first six years at Epic, I logged more and more time in the studio—always as an observer. I witnessed a few good production moves and a whole lot more that weren't so good. *This producer doesn't know what he's doing*, I'd say to myself. To me, what he should have done was obvious, but he just didn't hear it.

I felt badly for the artists, whose records suffered due to unimaginative and uninspired production. I wanted to spend more time in the studio, and I was certain that I could make good records. No other position in any profession looked as good as the record producer's chair. To be in the studio day and night, making good songs better with a band whose music you enjoyed, and to be well paid for this? This had to be the best job in the world.

Thanks to the first Ted Nugent session, I became a record producer without actually trying. I'd been toiling for five years, trying to sign bands, doing edits for single releases, and evaluating thousands of tapes and live performances—all with not much to show for it. Then, in a matter of weeks, I'd magically become a respected professional. There's so little consideration for experience in the record business that it really comes down to, 'What have you done for me this week?'

By the time I had finished co-producing Ted's third LP, I'd learned enough to make a decent album on my own. When Ted's debut went gold, the Epic brass were delighted; now they were happy to let me spend as much time as I wanted in the studio.

This hard-earned 'overnight' success wasn't so unusual in the robust record business of the 70s. The demand for a constant supply of new music helped a lot of novice producers and engineers to become established very quickly, as there were hardly enough of them to make all the records that music fans wanted to buy. Six years of frustration—and suddenly it went from, *Werman, what exactly do you do?* to *Werman! You're beautiful, babe!*

SIDE C
LIFE IN THE FAST LANE

CHAPTER THIRTEEN

WELCOME TO LA

I knew nothing about Los Angeles when I attended our big CBS Records convention there at the Century Plaza Hotel in Century City in July of 1976. It was my first time in the city, and even as an allegedly sophisticated New Yorker, I was wide-eyed. Century City was a 176-acre mini-city of tall office buildings, fountains, plazas, stores, restaurants, theaters—the whole complex appeared spotless and new, and unlike anything I'd seen back east.

Beverly Hills High School bordered Century City on one side, with a working oil well next to the running track, and the LA Country Club sat right across Santa Monica Boulevard, clearly visible from the hotel and the high twin-tower office buildings. We didn't get much time away from the hotel during those conventions, so Century City and the airport represented the extent of my familiarity with LA until I returned the following year with Cheap Trick.

The band wanted to record *In Color* in Los Angeles. Never having recorded there, I researched the studio situation and booked the Record Plant on Third Street. It was owned and operated by the same people who owned the Record Plant in Manhattan, one of the few studios I had spent time in. Rose Mann Cherney, the wonderful studio manager at the Record Plant, arranged everything for us, and also, very fortunately, introduced me to recording engineer Gary Ladinsky.

Life in Los Angeles was very different from life in New York in so many ways. In Manhattan, one could usually identify important or successful people by the clothes they wore. Wealthy people appeared wealthy because of their fine threads; the not-so-affluent appeared appropriately less splendid. Not so in LA.

I became fond of the Palm restaurant for business lunches. It was a favorite gathering spot for music people, and one day, a few months after I started dining there, David Geffen came in wearing jeans, tennis sneakers without socks, and a plain white t-shirt. He was clearly the most casually dressed person in the room. I was surprised to see him dressed this way, but the logic came to me right away. In New York, anyone of his stature would be dressed in a handmade, well-tailored suit, but in LA, the message was clear: 'I don't have to dress to impress—I'm important enough not to have to consider my appearance.'

In New York, I had worn jeans and boots to work. With my long hair, I stood out a little in the Midtown area, and especially in the CBS Building, because while I looked as if I belonged at a construction site, I actually had a nice office in one of the most powerful and important business centers in the world. In LA, however, no one could tell who you were from your appearance. It was one big masquerade ball. A far more accurate indication of your station in life was the vehicle you drove.

Someone had told me about a budget car-rental place at the corner of Third Street and La Cienega Boulevard, one long block down from the studio. It was one of several car rental offices in Hollywood that specialized in sporty or unusual automobiles. After all, if you're renting a car in a town where you are what you drive, you should choose a car that reflects your livelihood—not just a Hertz Chevy. One could even rent a Rolls-Royce or a Bentley right there on Wilshire Boulevard.

My LA rental choice was an Alfa Romeo Spider convertible, which went for a very reasonable $25 per day in 1975. The owner of the business was a young hustler who appeared to be quite taken with the showbiz life. When he learned I was in the music business, he quietly offered to provide a gram of cocaine in the glove box with each of my rentals. I was pleased with this arrangement, which went on for a few years until the poor guy was busted.

RIGHT My first real rock'n'roll band, playing on the patio of the Columbia University Student Union, fall 1963. Where are the Barnard girls from across the street? **BELOW** Three of the four members of The Walkers, my college band for three years, specializing in cover versions of The Beatles, Stones, and Byrds. *Left to right*: lead guitarist extraordinaire Billy Cross, myself on rhythm guitar, Adam Tepper on bass.

260 Riverside Drive
New York, New York 10025
September 9, 1970

Mr. Clive Davis
Columbia Broadcasting System
51 West 52 Street
New York, New York

Dear Mr. Davis:

Al Lewis at MGM urged me to write directly to you, since he felt you would be interested in my background. I would very much like to speak to you in person, so I will keep this note brief and introductory.

I earned a Masters Degree at Columbia Business School, following four years at the College. During my six years at Columbia, I led two very successful rock groups. On graduating, I passed up offers from a number of organizations, including yours and Procter & Gamble, in order to work at Grey Advertising to gain some marketing experience.

I am an Assistant Account Executive on a large Procter & Gamble account, and while my future at Grey is all but mapped out, my head is not. Despite all the talk about the tight job market, I am too involved with rock music to continue working outside the medium with any satisfaction, and I want to speak with you about combining my marketing and musical background in a more creative position at Columbia, whose work I greatly admire.

I will call your office Monday, September 14, so that we might set up an appointment for that week. I am looking forward to meeting with you.

Very sincerely,

Thomas Werman

CBS RECORDS
A Division of Columbia Broadcasting System, Inc.
51 West 52 Street
New York, New York 10019
(212) 765-4321

Walter L. Dean
Administrative Vice President

September 28, 1970

Mr. Thomas Werman
260 Riverside Drive
New York, N.Y. 10025

Dear Mr. Werman:

Bruce Lundvall spoke to me about his discussion with you.

If you are still interested in coming with Columbia, please telephone my secretary, Mrs. O'Grady, on Extension 4891, to arrange an appointment for us to discuss the matter further.

Very truly yours,

Walter L. Dean

WLD:do'g

OPPOSITE My letter to Clive Davis, requesting a job interview—a bit cheeky on my part, since I basically informed him that we would set the date for such a meeting when I phoned him on Monday of the following week.

ABOVE After several months and about five interviews, the letter I was waiting for arrived from the VP of business affairs at CBS Records; this led to my meeting with Clive Davis.

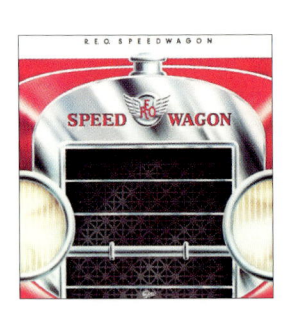

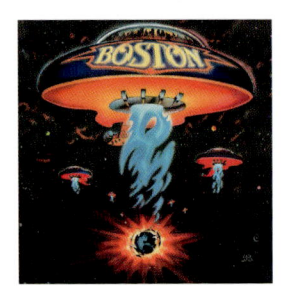

TOP Platinum awards for REO Speedwagon's 'You Can Tune A Piano But You Can't Tuna Fish.' *Left to right*: manager John Baruck, bassist Bruce Hall, label head Don Dempsey, drummer Alan Gratzer, guitarist Gary Richrath, Epic's Becky Mancuso-Winding, myself, singer Kevin Cronin, and keyboardist Neal Doughty. **ABOVE** A young A&R executive with a full head of hair. **LEFT** Debut album covers for REO and Boston.

CBS MEMORANDUM

let's discuss this!

LC

FROM: T. Werman
TO: L. COHN
DATE: February 25, 1971

Larry, I have firmed up my opinion of R.E.O. Speedwagon to the point where I think we should move directly to acquire some of their material, and preferably to sign the group itself, based on their writing/recording ability and supported by what I am guessing will be a very favorable report on their live act. This is a good rocking group; twice what "Catfish" ever tried to be.

"Gypsy Woman's Passion", "157 Riverside Avenue", and "Sophisticated Lady" are outstanding in their various genres, and the individual musicianship is superior. It looks like this act can meet the "star" qualifications that Columbia/EPIC likes to find in its groups. Let's find out what they want, for starters.

Thank you.

TW/meb

Tom

P.S. The mix on these acetates could be improved - and it still sounds better than a lot of finished albums.

ABOVE A memo to my boss, the head of A&R at Epic Records, leading to my first business trip to see REO Speedwagon live—and the first of my six signings in twelve years at the label.

T. Werman
L. COHN   bcc: D. Ellis
April 19, 1972

<u>Lynyrd Skynard</u>

As you requested, I went to Macon, Georgia last Thursday to hear the group Lynyrd Skynard.

The group consists of two lead guitars, bass, vocalist, and two drummers; there was only one drum set on hand, so the drummers alternated sets. The strength of this group is really in the two guitarists, who work beautifully together much the same as the Allmans (obviously, the group is patterned after them), but who inject a good deal more hard rock into the arrangements than do the Allmans. The vocalist is good, but does not add anything exceptional. The bass is very, very strong and has fine taste.

The group's material, though well arranged and interesting to hear live, is not commercial in the top 40 sense. However, the group's playing is so exceptional that I feel they are simply too good to pass up. Their live act is as tight as any I have seen, and the combination of hard rock with the Allmans' intricate style works well.

Naturally, with material such as theirs, their touring is of primary importance; Alan Walden said he was talking to Al de Marino, Johnny Podell and Frank Barsalona. I think you should definitely see the group yourself before closing any deal, since there seems to be so much bad blood between Walden and Becket. I told Walden to deal with you if he had any questions. Separate from that, it would be smart not to lock them into Muscle Shoals for production, because an independent producer could do wonders with this group, and they <u>should</u> work with a producer who can furnish them with the right material. Right now ther're excellent--with the right songs, they would be even stronger.

TW:rs

```
georgia 31201

May 9, 1972

Tom Werman
Epic Records
51 West 52nd Street
New York, N.Y. 10019

Dear Tom:

Atlanta was a gas. Both Associated Booking and William Morris had
representatives to come from New York and we knocked their heads off.
We have them booked into a club in Nashville for two weeks beginning
May 16. After this I have been promised several concert dates along
with a number of better clubs.

We drew twice the number of people than on our first trip to Atlanta.
The owner wants to reschedule now but I am in the process of setting
a concert date first. For our club work we are adding a Hammond B3.
Our new drummer will sing and play organ for the earlier sets, then
play drums when our lead vocalist sings.

I am sure now if we had our album out we would sell the product.

Enclosed is our newsletter from Grants and I'll send you the one from
Funnichio's. Will Don Ellis be able to come to Nashville?

Awaiting your reply, I remain,

Sincerely,

Alan Walden
HUSTLERS, INC.

AW/bw

Encls.

(912) 742-0932
```

OPPOSITE A memo to outgoing A&R head Larry Cohn and incoming A&R head Don Ellis, urging Don to sign Skynyrd to the label; he passed.

ABOVE The Epic Records A&R staff, 1973: Stephen Paley, Diane Hyatt, department head Don Ellis, Gregg Geller, and yours truly. **LEFT** A letter from Alan Walden of Capricorn Records, manager of Lynyrd Skynyrd, following my trip to see them live in Macon, Georgia.

CBS MEMORANDUM

FROM: Tom Werman
TO: SEE LIST
DATE: June 1, 1973

Re: Manhattan Transfer

Regarding the attached memo which was circulated a month ago, the concert which the group wanted to substitute for the audition is scheduled for Friday, June 8th at the Diplomat Hotel on West 43rd Street, just off 6th Avenue. The group will follow a brief opening act, and should perform at 10:30.

Much of the group's material goes back to the early forties; the arrangements of that era with today's instrumentation and sound technology make for an interesting combination which adds still another dimension to the Midler School.

Please let me know if you would like to attend, so I can arrange for a list if necessary.

Tom

TW/ja

TO: ALTSHULER   HANDWERGER   OBERMAN
    ANDON   HARRIS, B.   PALEY
    COHEN   HARRIS, S.   POPOVICH
    COFFINO   KLENFNER   PROFFER
    DOBBIS   KRUGMAN   SEGELSTEIN
    DEVITO   LIEBERSON   SHARGO
    EICHNER   LOURIE   SLUTZAH
    ELLIS   LOVE   SPECTOR
    GARNER   LUNDVALL   TELLER
    GELLER   McCARRELL   TYRRELL
    HAMMOND   MONTEIRO   WENRICK

ABOVE A memo from me to some of the Columbia Records staff urging them to go see Manhattan Transfer, because I thought the group was better suited to Columbia than to Epic. No one from that cc list followed my suggestion. Shortly thereafter, the group signed to Atlantic Records.

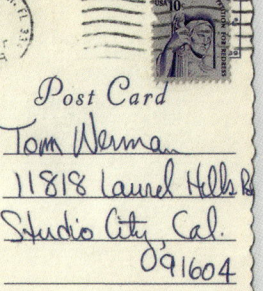

TOP Receiving awards for sales of over a million copies of Ted's debut Epic LP, *Ted Nugent*. Left to right: drummer Cliff Davies, co-producer Lew Futterman, Ted, and myself. Courtesy Sony Music Archives/ photograph by Roz Levin.

ABOVE The first three Ted Nugent album covers.

LEFT A postcard from Ted telling me how pleased he was with the first record.

ABOVE The New York and LA Epic A&R staff, 1977: Ron Alexenburg, Lennie Petze, Gregg Geller, Steve Popovich, Becky Mancuso-Winding, John Boylan, myself, Al Aronowitz, and Sam Lederman.

BELOW The New York, Los Angeles, and Nashville Epic A&R staff at a Palm Springs retreat in 1978: Bruce Harris, Frank Rand, Mike Atkinson, Larry Schnur, Lennie Petze, Don Dempsey, Bonnie Garner, Bobby Colomby, John Boylan, Russell Timmons, myself, Doreen Courtright, Andi Stevens, Becky Mancuso-Winding, Kelly Traynor.

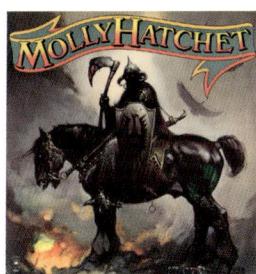

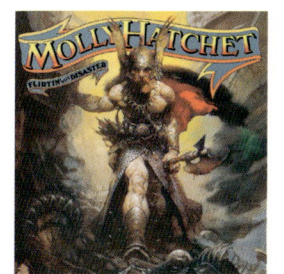

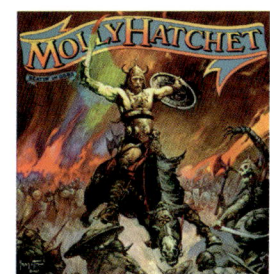

TOP An unlikely trio at a cocktail reception: crooner Rudy Vallee, Molly Hatchet guitarist Dave Hlubek, and myself, 1979.
ABOVE The first three platinum Molly Hatchet albums.
RIGHT Working at Beejay Studios in Orlando, amused by recording engineer Geoff Workman's antics, 1983.

RIGHT Myself holding daughter Julia, my wife Suky, and Cheap Trick's Rick Nielsen, 1978. **BELOW** The three Cheap Trick albums I produced. **BOTTOM** *Back row*: product manager Jim Charne, myself, Epic's Al DeMarino, and Cheap Trick's Robin, Tom, Rick and Bun E. Carlos. *Front row*: promotion man Alan Ostroff, manager Ken Adamany, and head of promotion Jim Jeffries.

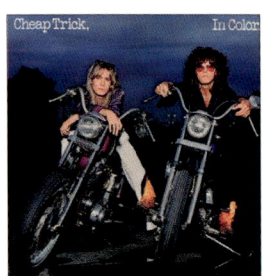

ABOVE Happy conventioneers, 1978: publicist Susan Blond, A&R man Gregg Geller, myself, Columbia's Peter Philbin, Epic A&R's John Boylan, and Columbia promotion man Terry Powell. *Courtesy Sony Music Archives/photograph by Roz Levin.* **LEFT** Jeff Beck and Epic label head Ron Alexenburg. *Courtesy Sony Music Archives.*

CBS MEMORANDUM

This is ridiculous! Dave Hlubeck deserves this gig, not you. Boy are we pissed!
Love it, my man! Best,

FROM: Bruce Lundvall (CRU)
TO: OFFICERS AND DEPARTMENT HEADS OF CBS/RECORDS GROUP, DIVISIONS AND SUBSIDIARIES
DATE: September 25, 1980

I am pleased to announce that Tom Werman has been appointed as Vice President/Executive Producer, CBS Records. In this exclusive arrangement, Mr. Werman, reporting to Gregg Geller, Vice President, National A&R, Epic Records, will seek out, evaluate and sign artists to the Epic label, and will concentrate on producing artists for the Epic, Columbia, Portrait and CBS Associated Labels, working closely with Mr. Geller as well as Mickey Eichner, Vice President, National A&R, Columbia Records; and Lennie Petze, Vice President and General Manager, Portrait Records.

Mr. Werman is regarded as one of the most successful producers and talent scouts in the record industry, and has produced eight Platinum and four Gold Records for Epic Records. He has signed such million-selling artists as Cheap Trick, Ted Nugent, Molly Hatchet and REO Speedwagon as well as Epic's Mother's Finest. Mr. Werman produced the album, "Mirrors" by Columbia recording group Blue Oyster Cult, and Gary Myrick's debut LP for Epic, "Gary Myrick and The Figures." He is currently in Los Angeles completing production on the debut album by Columbia's The Hawks.

Since 1977, Mr. Werman has served as Staff Producer, Epic Records. He joined the Label in 1971 as Assistant to the Director, A&R, and in 1973 became Director, Talent Acquisition. Prior to coming to Epic, Mr. Werman worked at Grey Advertising as Account Executive.

Mr. Werman holds a B.A. degree from Columbia College and an M.B.A. degree from Columbia Business School.

OPPOSITE A promotional announcement from CBS Records president Bruce Lundvall, topped by some trash talk from my friend and Epic colleague Bruce Harris.

RIGHT Members of Brownsville (Station) with myself and recording engineer Gary Ladinsky at the remote recording session of their album *Air Special* in Ann Arbor, Michigan; Epic A&R department head Steve Popovich handing me an award at a CBS Records convention, 1978. **BELOW** The broadly grinning producer, The Producers guitarist Van Temple, Epic label head Don Dempsey, and Producers drummer Bryan Holmes. *Courtesy Sony Music Archives/photograph by Roz Levin.*

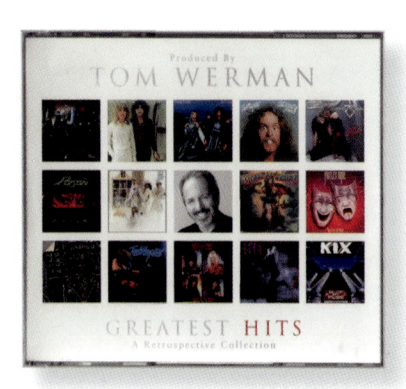

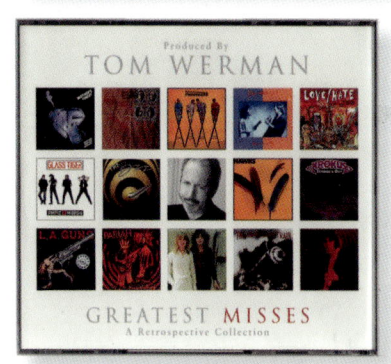

ABOVE Both sides of my two-CD set *Greatest Hits & Greatest Misses*, a memoir containing the hits on one disc, and on the other disc the best of my productions that I considered overlooked or under-promoted. I put this together when I retired from the music industry. **RIGHT** The happy Stonover Farm innkeeper manicuring his ten-acre property in Lenox, Massachusetts (The Berkshires); with ZZ Top guitar hero Billy Gibbons, one of my favorites, at a rehearsal studio in Palm Springs, 2023.

CHAPTER THIRTEEN | 113

During the *In Color* project, I stayed in a poolside suite at the Sunset Marquis, just off Sunset Boulevard in Hollywood. In the 70s, this was a modestly priced, funky hangout for rockers—a hotel that not only tolerated musicians but welcomed and catered to them. Half of the hotel's rooms surrounded the pool, and it was always interesting to see who was out there. Today, it's still one of the best places in town for musicians to stay—far, far more expensive but very comfortable, with print ads that boasted, 'If we were any more Hollywood, our pool would be shallow at both ends' and 'Rooms so beautiful, even the most demented rock stars don't have the heart to trash them.'

This became my home away from home in LA, and I always requested the same suite, right on the pool, where the big sliding glass doors were just a few steps from the water. On a day off during the *In Color* sessions, I took a walk up to Sunset Boulevard. It was a perfect day with bright sun, deep blue sky, and warm, dry air. I stopped to survey the window at North Beach Leather and admire the embroidered suits, all hand-stitched in Mexico. A few years later, I'd return to purchase a couple of these suits, which I wore to concerts or clubs. With the 'all-access' laminate hanging from around my neck, the outfit made a nice 'music guy backstage' statement. It was a long way from the Brooks Brothers navy blazer and striped tie I had to wear to prep school in Boston, and while I can laugh about it now, I thought those leather suits were pretty cool back then.

As I strolled down Sunset Boulevard on that idle Sunday, it dawned on me that I could actually *live* in Los Angeles if I wanted to. It would involve a major lifestyle change, and when we did eventually make the move, many of my childhood friends were puzzled by our decision. 'Why on earth would you do that?' they asked. Though they tended to be well-educated, Bostonians were fairly provincial, and they weren't all that interested in investigating life outside of the greater Boston area.

In the Boston Jewish community, being adventurous meant moving a few miles away from the suburbs where you grew up. Leaving the eastern urban corridor was a big deal, and something that was rarely considered.

I was motivated to make the move by a moment in the studio when Rick Nielsen wanted to use an electric sitar on one song, and I had no idea how to get one. Our assistant engineer said, 'I'll call Studio Instrument Rentals.' I'd never heard of a company that was in business just to supply studios with rental instruments and recording equipment, but in about twenty minutes, S.I.R. had delivered to our control room a perfectly tuned Coral electric sitar. This was a real eye-opener. I realized there was a whole industry in LA that was dedicated to serving the various needs of the music business. In New York, entertainment didn't even make the top fifteen of the biggest industries. In LA, it was number one.

This was clearly the most convenient place in the world to make records. Add the weather, the palm trees, the beach, the fine restaurants, the beautiful people, life in the fast lane, and it was a no-brainer: we needed to move to Los Angeles right away.

* * *

Epic Records was very accommodating. When I told them I'd be happier making records in LA, they supported the move completely, and we began to make plans. I would have an office in the Carlsberg Building, Epic's home just across the street from Century City; CBS would pay for all our moving expenses, give us a new appliance allowance, pay for a few weeks of car rentals, and put us up at the hotel of our choice. Once again, I chose the Sunset Marquis, where CBS gave us a spacious suite for the whole family until the house was ready.

We bought a home in Studio City, just off fabled Laurel Canyon

Boulevard. Studio City was a family-oriented section of LA, and our house was about a mile down the hill from Mulholland Drive. It was quite a change for a family who had come from a gray, three-bedroom stucco house in Leonia, New Jersey.

Laurel Canyon had a lot of rock'n'roll history—CSNY, the Eagles, Joni Mitchell, The Byrds, The Doors, The Monkees, Frank Zappa—but by 1978, it had pretty much reverted to a regular gorge through the Santa Monica mountain range, with a generous number of hippies living on the Hollywood side. The Laurel Canyon artists who had made it big in the early 70s had all headed west to Santa Monica, Brentwood, Malibu, Pacific Palisades, and especially Beverly Hills. After 1975, if you crossed Mulholland and headed down into the San Fernando Valley, Laurel Canyon was strictly suburban family territory.

Our house was at the end of a cul-de-sac, and just over the backyard fence was the Tom Mix ranch. Few Angelenos knew much about Tom Mix, the biggest silent-screen cowboy in Hollywood during the 1920s. The last remaining tract of his once-sprawling ranch comprised the view from our house and backyard. Sitting by the pool, we'd look over corrals, sagebrush, and a horse barn, all the way up to Mulholland Drive. It was a brand new world—4,500 square feet, five bedrooms, four bathrooms, an office, a den, and a garage that I converted to a 'media room' with one of the first big-screen projection TVs on the market. We had a nice yard, a carport, a great pool, and people to take care of it all. We actually converted to solar for hot water in the early 80s.

An Epic colleague of mine had been helpful in getting us set up in our new home in the Canyon, and we became friendly with her and her boyfriend. As she learned how to advance in the world of show business, she developed the distracting habit of looking over your shoulder when chatting at an event, to see if there was anyone around who was more important. If there was, she'd excuse herself, and off she'd go to chat up her prey. If there was no one worthy of her attention, she might continue your conversation, keeping a watchful eye on the door.

As I made more hit records, I grew accustomed to the glitz and conspicuous consumption in LA. I traded my East Coast Datsun for a 911 Porsche to go along with those cool hand-stitched leather suits from North Beach Leather; in other words, I adopted some of LA's less admirable cultural values. During the time we lived in Laurel Canyon, I had two Porsches. Being young, affluent, and impressionable, I ordered vanity plates for each of them—one read 'HVYMETL' and the other '33RPM.' I thought this was clever, since they referred to both my profession and the car at the same time.

I did, however, try to retain a few social values I had learned on the East Coast, even though they weren't always appreciated. The first time I stood up when a woman approached the table, the fellow seated next to me asked where I was going. After a few months in town, I managed to discard some of my 'newbie' insecurities—one day, I pulled up to the light at the five-way intersection on Sunset near the Beverly Hills Hotel, feeling pretty cool in my recently purchased Porsche, when a Ferrari pulled up next to me. I realized then that it was fruitless to try to compete in this town because there would always be someone who's better dressed, drives a cooler car, makes much more money, and is more successful. After that, I was able to relax a little and enjoy our new life in Tinseltown.

Another way New York and Los Angeles differed: it was harder to be a pretender or poser in LA. You couldn't conceal your failures the way someone like Trump could in New York; LA was simply a sprawling suburb, and if you had any visibility at all, everyone in entertainment knew who you were, where you lived, where your kids went to school, what you drove, where you bought your clothes and your meals, who your close friends were, how well your last movie, book, record, or performance did, and probably what your net worth was. It was no longer the hippie playground it once was, back when New Yorkers regarded it as being in the minor leagues and thought that making it there was a piece of cake.

In the 1970s, you would approach a stoplight and four cars would be lined up in the right lane, with none in the left. A local Angeleno would follow the car in front of him and become the fifth car in the right lane, while an Eastern transplant would zip into the first spot in the left lane. By the mid-80s, the no-rush, laid-back attitude had all but vanished.

Professionally, things went well for me in Los Angeles. Life was far less costly than it had been in New York, and I was collecting a good CBS salary as well as a growing amount of royalty money from my records. By this time, CBS had exhausted all the appropriate job titles for an unusual position like mine, so the official title on my company-issued business card was 'Senior Vice President / Executive Producer.' I was still an A&R man, with all the accompanying duties and privileges, but I was a staff producer as well. I had an office and a secretary at the label offices in Century City, but when I was doing a record I'd come into the office only once or twice a week. I attended almost no meetings, yet I still had a generous expense account. Because the record business was so healthy in the late 70s and early 80s, and because I'd been with the company for eleven years, my expense report was never questioned, and I paid for very few meals out.

When Suky and the kids came down to the studio for dinner, we'd go out to a nice restaurant—sometimes with and sometimes without a member of the act I was working with. On the expense report, I'd put the artist's name in the 'reason' column. Many label people with an expense account did this routinely. One department head organized a big working dinner for staff members from both coasts and Nashville, and he quietly had the waiter put a case of expensive wine in the trunk of his limo. This would get lost in the dinner bill, which could easily approach a couple of thousand dollars, even in the 1980s.

Some producers were known to buy drugs for themselves and the band and have the album budget pay for it by entering it on the studio budget as 'recording tape.' Two-inch tape cost hundreds of dollars per reel, and projects could easily fill between ten and twenty reels. I never did this. Fudging dinners on my expense report defined the extent of my white-collar crime.

CHAPTER FOURTEEN

(MOLLY) HATCHET JOB

Named after an eighteenth-century prostitute who allegedly beheaded her lovers ('Hatchet Molly'), Molly Hatchet traveled north from their native Jacksonville to audition for me at the Sound Pit in Atlanta in 1977. I was there remixing Cheap Trick's 'Southern Girls,' which Epic wanted to release as a single. The Hatchet boys set up in the studio while I was mixing in the control room, and engineer Tony Reale and I took a break from the mix to hear their set.

This was a rough-looking crew—something visually to the left of Lynyrd Skynyrd. The band's leader, Dave Hlubek, was missing one of his front teeth; heavy drinking and smoking had already etched lines into each of their young faces, and they looked like they loved to brawl for fun. Turns out they really did. But the music they played was sublime: a tight, harmony-filled, three-guitar attack that brought me back to my roadhouse experience in Macon, Georgia, several years earlier.

Following their surprisingly strong performance, I expressed my enthusiasm to the band.

'Mr. Werman,' Dave replied, laughing, 'I just want my front tooth back.'

I signed them immediately, and over the following months I developed a solid relationship with their straight-edge manager, Pat Armstrong. Pat was a smart, churchgoing, buttoned-down real-estate entrepreneur with a cheerful nature and a talent for making money. He clearly enjoyed the unusual diversion that Hatchet offered him. I was his frequent house guest, and he seemed happy to find someone involved with the band who could sit down, have a few drinks, use the proper utensils for each course, and carry on a reasonable conversation.

Pat had made a deal with the owner of a modest studio close to both my hotel and his house in suburban Orlando. We recorded four out of our five Molly Hatchet albums there. All five sold over a million copies. The biggest was *Flirtin' With Disaster*, which did over three million.

Engineer Gary Ladinsky and I would fly into Orlando from LA on a Monday morning, spend the week recording, then take the midnight plane back to LA on Friday night. This way, we could fly first class for coach fare, and after a week with Hatchet, every little comfort made a difference. Our hotel was an ancient relic in cozy Winter Park, an old-money suburb of Orlando and the home of Rollins College. The rooms were shabbily furnished, but they had air-conditioning and high ceilings, and they cost under $100 per night. There was a new bar/restaurant and a wonderful swimming pool. We'd spend the mornings by the pool, have lunch at the restaurant, and go to the studio just after lunch. It wasn't exactly a vacation, but on many days it felt like one.

The bar was host to a number of elderly locals who were given little paddles with numbers on them; when you wanted another round, you simply raised your paddle. Some folks would spend this inherited old money on cocktails in air-conditioned comfort for the entire afternoon. For most of the year, the Orlando area weather could best be described as sultry.

The band drank hard, and they loved to fight. Their idea of a good time after work was to go to a bar, do a couple of lines, suck down some Jack Daniel's, and then empty the place of patrons. They always made it a point to invite me along, and I always made it a point to graciously decline.

I was told that the guitar player, Duane Roland, had been shot in the stomach by his father. Only drummer Bruce Crump didn't have the street-smart, tough-guy appearance. He was a prep-school boy gone wrong—like me. Singer Danny Joe Brown, a big friendly guy, was diabetic, and he would tailor his insulin injections so that he could quaff his full measure of bourbon. They enjoyed prodigious amounts of cocaine, washed down by a lot of Jack Daniel's and chased with a shot or two of Jägermeister. Florida cocaine was of a higher quality than LA cocaine—and it was considerably cheaper.

One day, Dave was late to the studio, and, after some calling around, manager Pat discovered that he'd been arrested for doing doughnuts behind the wheel of his Corvette Stingray in a public parking lot. The boys loved to play games.

Our studio was owned and operated by a quiet, born-again young couple; he was handsome and soft-spoken, and she was a stunning, willowy girl of no more than twenty-five with straight blonde hair down to below her waist. Being devout Christians, they had converted one of the rooms in the studio building to a chapel, complete with several rows of pews and a stained-glass window.

On one hot spring day, this pretty, innocent-looking young married girl decided to accompany some of the Hatchet road-crew guys on a day trip to Disney World. The head roadie was a skinny fellow with big ears. He was personable and a bit odd looking, and the band had dubbed him 'Jughead,' or 'Juggie' for short. The following morning, I learned that he and the pretty wife had run off together. We never saw them again. The band found this amusing but not terribly unusual. I was absolutely bowled over by the whole thing, and later that day I sat in the control room wondering exactly how a nice Jewish boy from Boston ever wound up in a situation like this.

Our fourth record was recorded in the Bahamas at a lovely place called Compass Point, owned and operated by Chris Blackwell, heir to the Crosse & Blackwell food company and founder/owner of Island Records. Robert Palmer ('Addicted To Love,' 'Simply Irresistible') would spend much of his time down there. The living quarters were just across the street from the studio, yards from the warm, blue-green Caribbean.

We'd spend the morning at the swimming pool, then record until about four in the afternoon, after which we'd stroll down the road a piece to the Traveler's Rest. There, we'd order up conch fritters and some goombay smashes—a potent local rum cocktail with a little umbrella. Then we'd go back and do our professional best until about nine in the evening. At that point we'd call it a day, dress up a little, and drive a few miles down the only road on that end of the island to the Playboy Club Casino.

This was certainly the most entertaining and pleasant recording environment I'd experienced. Talking Heads' Chris Franz and Tina Weymouth were also at the studio, working on their Tom Tom Club project, so when I grew tired of the drinking, swearing, smoking, and fighting with Molly Hatchet, I could seek these two out to have a stimulating conversation.

Sadly, the Compass Point studio complex was closed in 2010. According to one of their websites, this came about 'because of a series of incidents—sociopolitical-based happenings which made it untenable to continue business in the Bahamas.' A damn shame.

During the Molly Hatchet recording sessions there, one of the guitar players suddenly decided to get married, so he summoned his family and friends from nearby Jacksonville, Florida. Waiting for the late-afternoon ceremony on the big day, he consumed an enormous amount of rum, and—already nursing a grudge against me for consistently giving him the smallest guitar role on the album (which I did because the other two players were better and more exciting), drunkenly fired off a couple of choice antisemitic slurs.

Not exactly sober at that moment either, I surprised myself by kicking off my flip-flops, assuming a casual karate stance, and quietly inviting him to give it his best shot. He backed down, turned, and walked away, and the incident never came up again. I felt pretty satisfied with myself, and Gary and I enjoyed a pleasant wedding.

Manager Pat Armstrong did quite well with Molly Hatchet. Regrettably, the band members put most of their newfound wealth up their noses. I later heard that Dave, who had been the proud owner of an Orlando lakeside mansion with two Rolls-Royces in the driveway, eventually lost it all. I don't think the others fared much better. This happened to quite a few bands, but fortunately I never saw it happen to any of my other clients. I had felt good about helping the Molly Hatchet guys to become financially comfortable, so it was disappointing to learn that, after selling millions of albums, they ended up falling on hard times.

Molly Hatchet stayed on the road for years; a band with their name was still touring recently, but all five original members have passed away—all much younger than I was. To know and work with them was a fascinating experience.

All in all, life was very good. At one point, I had three albums by different bands in the Top 40 of the *Billboard* album chart. I remember one day, driving to the Record Plant when 'Flirtin' With Disaster' came on the radio; normally, I'd listen closely to any of my songs when I heard them on the radio, but this time I pulled into the studio parking lot and exited the car before the song ended, knowing I'd probably hear another one of my songs on the way home. At one of our conventions at the Century Plaza Hotel, I was presented with my first two gold records onstage during the twelve-hundred-person dinner show in the grand ballroom—one for Ted Nugent and one for Cheap Trick. I made a few comments and then walked through the ballroom, up the escalator to the lobby elevator with a gold record under each arm. I felt a little awkward but also very important, and I partied hard that night.

CHAPTER FIFTEEN

THE STUDIO: SANCTUM SANCTORUM

In the 70s, the CBS Records studio complex on Manhattan's 52nd Street was an all-purpose recording facility, designed to service any genre of music. Artists as different from one another as Journey, Tony Bennett, and Miles Davis could use the same studio room successfully in one twenty-four-hour period. Dylan and a host of musical legends recorded there too, but in the early 70s other 'all-purpose' New York recording studios had already started to undergo modification and were being redesigned and outfitted specifically for rock'n'roll.

Studio features that attracted rock bands included the latest outboard gear for processing sound in new and different ways; a rich old Leslie speaker cabinet for the organ or guitar or vocals; a high-quality piano (I preferred Yamahas to Steinways for recording); a collection of vintage guitars and amps; a large selection of microphones; specific devices to alter or process the sounds of vocals or stringed instruments; high-powered, full-range control-room monitors; a few pairs of good smaller speakers for mixing; and, later, a warm-sounding, computerized recording console.

I first noticed the change at Jimi Hendrix's Electric Lady Studios on 8th Street in the West Village, and at the midtown Record Plant when I visited the control room for a couple of Jack Douglas's sessions. These re-designed studios had a very different vibe from CBS's studios. They offered versatile lighting, recording devices that more accurately served the particular needs of the rock musician, and the requisite comforts and conveniences provided for the rock'n'roll human. Control rooms became more like living rooms; there were reclining, rolling leather chairs for the engineer and producer, a lounge with video games and ping-pong tables, and kitchens with refrigerators, ice machines, espresso makers, and microwave ovens.

By contrast, the 52nd Street CBS studio building didn't provide a single lounge for its clients, and there were only a couple of vending machines for coffee and unhealthy snacks. There were no sofas in the control rooms; it was all business.

The more desirable studios became so by acquiring a discreet knowledge of the producer's lifestyle, desires, and work habits, and they did whatever was necessary in order to turn their studio into that producer's personal comfort zone. Where serious musicians like Miles or Sinatra or Simon & Garfunkel approached the recording studio as a workplace, rockers were more self-indulgent, and a growing number saw the studio as a private party room where they could spend time with their friends and make music only when the spirit moved them. Very few of the rock'n'roll sessions I witnessed or conducted were attended by just the essential personnel (band, producer, recording engineer, and assistant engineer). There were always visitors—mostly at night, and mostly female.

I got a glimpse of the future in the mid-70s when the Epic A&R department held a retreat at the Caribou Ranch, Jim Guercio's mountaintop studio in Nederland, Colorado. Jim managed and produced the Columbia band Chicago, and this was where they recorded. I was amazed at the size and scope of the place—the ranch buildings were surrounded by thousands of wilderness acres, and, due to the elevation, there was a row of oxygen tanks in the studio for the horn players.

Elton John recorded *Caribou* at the Ranch, and The Beach Boys and Joe Walsh also made LP's there. The complex had plush living quarters—spacious log cabins with large living rooms, pinball machines, pool tables, TVs, stereos, and kitchens—all designed to make musicians feel as comfortable as possible while they were away from home. If you wanted to take a break from recording, in the winter you could take off on a snowmobile, and in summer you could take off on a horse. The complex was staffed mostly by attractive young women who cooked and served the meals and generally took care of the artists' needs.

I learned a lot from Tony Reale, the first engineer I worked with at the Atlanta Sound Pit. I had originally met him a few years earlier at CBS's 52nd Street studio in New York, while he was mixing Johnny Nash's 'I Can See Clearly Now.' That mixing session was an eye-opener for me: I watched Tony review sixteen different recorded tracks, tweak the sound and character of each, combine them together, and ultimately paint a musical canvas from extreme right to extreme left, adjusting the volume of each one to achieve a cohesive, living, breathing musical experience. It was a difficult process, but Tony made it look easy. A scant few weeks later, I watched the song zoom up the charts to #1. After that, being a record producer became my singular obsession.

A recording studio is the producer's kingdom. In the 70s, a producer would select the studio he wanted to use, and the record label would authorize a payment of as much as $3,000 a day to rent the facility. The studio served the producer's every need. You ruled your little realm; when you arrived for work, you could have lunch waiting for you, and you'd tell the front desk who was allowed through the door to visit and whose phone calls they should put through (otherwise, they took messages and delivered them to your control room).

Of the many recording studios I used, two studios figured largely in my LA-based projects: the Record Plant and Conway Recorders.

The Record Plant was founded by Gary Kellgren and Chris Stone, two gentlemen whose lifestyles were at opposite ends of the behavioral spectrum. Kellgren died at an early age from excessive partying, at which point Chris Stone became the sole head of the studio, maintaining a fine balance between his dual roles as a sharp, effective, and savvy executive (primary) and a confidante and facilitator to his clients (secondary).

Chris was a wonderful guy—he'd help you to solve any problem that might arise, and if he could make things more comfortable for you, he did. He understood the rock'n'roll attitude well, but at the same time, he ran a tight ship that turned a handsome profit. Studio manager Rose kept the studio humming and packed with clients, and she could arrange just about anything you wanted, any time, day or night. She attracted a lot of business with a lot of prestigious artists, had a firm grip on the business side of the studio, and could party with the best.

The Record Plant was a fraternity. The producers and engineers who worked there a lot comprised a brotherhood whose members lived in a world about which mere mortals knew very little. On one particularly indulgent evening in studio B, sometime after midnight, visitors and musicians alike were draped over the couch and the recording console, fairly spent from excessive partying; but there stood our diligent assistant engineer Mike Beiriger, ignoring the chaos and carefully annotating and boxing up the master tapes before returning them to the vault—an example of the Plant's rare party / professional combination. Chris and Rose carefully trained and assigned these assistant engineers to act as professional ringmasters who facilitated, maintained, and controlled the perpetual circus.

* * *

'Runners' were essential to the smooth operation of a recording studio. They were there to clean bathrooms, sweep floors, do odd jobs, and run errands; they were employed by the studio, but they worked for the clients. I tried not to abuse this privilege, but after I'd become a regular at the Record Plant, I would call in my lunch order just before I left the house. That way, I'd arrive at work and my lunch would be waiting for me in the lounge, courtesy of the runner—and the fries were very well done, just as I requested.

Depending on the power and status of the client, the runner could pick up your dry cleaning, fetch drugs from a dealer, or take your car to get a full tank of gas. A good runner did all this as quickly, quietly, and efficiently as possible.

When not running errands or being otherwise occupied, a runner would stand in the rear of the control room and observe. Ambitious and capable runners became assistant engineers; this was the standard way up. You'd start as a custodian, making coffee, sweeping floors, and cleaning bathrooms; then graduate to gopher (runner), become an assistant engineer, and eventually be promoted to recording engineer, attached to—and exclusive to—the studio that gave you your start. If you then achieved a certain level of success, you could be an independent engineer for hire at any studio.

Many engineers became conversant with a variety of recording rooms and would be comfortable working in any number of different studios. A successful 'house' engineer was a valuable studio asset. I used five engineers over fifty-two album projects and recorded in about fifteen different studios over that time, but my comfort zone and my real home away from home was the Record Plant. Toward the end of my career, the Record Plant was sold. It re-opened across town with a more modern, straighter vibe—more work, less partying—its vibe changing along with the attitude of the industry.

After that, I began to use Conway Recorders, down Melrose Avenue toward East LA. Conway was a fenced-in complex of two studios with a fine mix room, an office building, a pool room, a kitchen, a common living room, a tech shop, a tape library, and a private lounge for each studio. All of this was within what could be described as a tropical paradise. Palms, fruit trees, and lush grasses bordered the studios, and a brick walk wound through the complex. We could have a meal, a beer, a joint, or just kick back on the porch or the patio right outside the studio.

There was a large parking lot with a basketball hoop and a nice lawn surrounded by gardens. Barbra Streisand brought a large Airstream trailer into the parking lot, apparently so she wouldn't have to socialize with the hoi polloi in the living room. She insisted on fresh flowers daily in her studio. We never saw her. Madonna, on the other hand, was accessible; she occasionally hung out in the lounge.

One day I arrived at the studio, pulled up to the security gate, and rang the buzzer. While I waited for someone to buzz me in, a car sped by on the street behind me with a man firing a gun repeatedly at someone on the street. I dove for the floor. This was not unusual for the neighborhood. A few years earlier, at the Record Plant, I was chatting with the front-desk attendant around midnight when two men in trench coats walked in the door. One of them took out a sawed-off shotgun and put it to my head.

'You and me are takin' a walk,' he said. He had come to collect a drug debt from another producer who wasn't in the studio at that time.

I pleaded ignorance, and very fortunately he left a minute later. It happened so quickly that I barely had time to panic. Also very fortunately, this was a rare, one-off encounter—an occupational hazard of life in the fast lane. Overall, though, considering the quality of life and the freedom afforded by the nature of the workplace, I was a very happy camper.

* * *

From my very first solo production job, Cheap Trick's *In Color*, I began to develop a comfortable and effective process that I'd use on most of my subsequent projects.

SELECTING THE SONGS: This was (I swear) a democratic process—a consensus formed between the band, the producer, the label A&R man, and sometimes even the manager. We would typically pick fourteen or fifteen songs, and then, as the recording progressed, we'd identify the weakest and strongest of the bunch and devote more time to the ones we thought might be single releases.

The producer is hired to work for the band. Consequently, the band can also fire him. Sometimes the label can force a producer on a band, but a producer cannot force anything on a band. In the case of an album I did with Krokus, the label actually gave us a song to record, and the label president assigned the task of lyric approval to their VP of business affairs. Seriously.

Dee Snider of Twisted Sister has insisted many times—falsely—that I 'refused' to do 'We're Not Gonna Take It,' and that I 'wouldn't allow' the band to cut a particular tune. This is pure fiction. The label has the last word. Period.

PRE-PRODUCTION: An effective record producer should 'join' the band for a couple of months. You can become friendly with the guys, but not too friendly—you need to maintain a measure of authority. It's okay to party with the band once in a while, too, but in moderation...

A good producer oversees, arranges, and directs just about everything that happens during the creation of a record, counseling, advising, collaborating, composing, evaluating, arranging, and sometimes even performing with the band.

Pre-production is an essential part of the project. The band supplied a demo of their songs and I listened to them many times. In the best of cases, one or two songs would emerge as potential hits. I'd make notes regarding structural changes or tweaks to drum parts, for instance, and we'd try these changes out in the rehearsal sessions. If we all liked them, we'd record the new version of the song on a portable cassette recorder at the rehearsal, then bring it with us to the studio, referring to it just before we rolled tape on the song.

In rehearsal, I always urged the drummer and bass player to try to play together as well as Fleetwood Mac's John McVie and Mick Fleetwood, whom I considered to be the tightest rhythm section in rock music. The pairing of Fleetwood Mac's drums and bass sounded like a single instrument.

I wouldn't rehearse any instrumental solos or vocals in pre-production because I wanted the musicians to retain some spontaneity in the studio. Too much rehearsal can make the song grow stale and dampen a musician's enthusiasm.

In order to hire the appropriate recording engineer for each project, a producer needed only to listen to that engineer's previous work, but in my case I got lucky and found Gary Ladinsky. Over the years, we'd end up making fifteen albums together.

I booked a different studio for each phase of the recording, from the basic tracks (usually drums, bass guitar, and rhythm guitars) to the final mix. At the start of a project, you need a big room in order to have the band play together and to provide isolation for each instrument; if you're the bass player, for example, your amp might sit in an isolation booth so that the sound of the drums doesn't leak into the microphone on the bass amp. This enables players to maintain eye contact and to be near each other, but also to have their own earphone mixes, so they can adjust the volume of their instruments while hearing all the other musicians.

On the first day in the studio, the engineer and I would set up all the players and instruments, and then we'd sit in the control room and dial in the right sound for each instrument. This might require spending more than an hour on one snare drum, or sampling five different snare drums, or maybe changing the snare drum skin multiple times until you've finally achieved that full *whomp* with a little percussive snap on top—you did whatever was necessary, and the process could be pretty tedious. (Sometimes I wouldn't enter the control room until the second day of setup, just so I didn't have to listen to the drummer hit the snare five hundred times in a row.)

LOAD-IN AND SETUP: Most bands initially insist on recording live, especially if it's their first studio experience. I would then try to explain to them why this might not be the best approach, but they would persist. To the band, not recording the album live would feel like something of a copout. But I much prefer recording one instrument at a time ('layering') for the purity of the sound that results.

Before a band has recorded in a studio, they'll only have experienced playing onstage at high volume, straining to hear the other musicians while struggling to hear themselves. A high-quality studio microphone picks up sounds that the human ear doesn't, however. It's like a sonic microscope. So I'd tell them that we'd record a couple of performances live, and then they could come back into the control room to listen to the result. In most cases, when the band members returned to the control room and heard their individual performances under the scrutiny of professional studio microphones, their enthusiasm for recording live vanished pretty quickly, and they'd agree that my way probably made more sense. Any performance error stuck out like a sore thumb; before we got halfway through the playback, the band would usually get the picture.

THE ALL-IMPORTANT RECORDING ENGINEER: I call myself a technoramus—I have zero aptitude for electronic devices, computers, or technology of any sort. For me to understand how to use something, it has to be very user-friendly, because I'm a very unfriendly user. Even well before the era of computerized recording, I was totally dependent on a competent and creative recording engineer who understood how to use the available technology to deliver what I wanted from the music.

Later on, in the late 80s and early 90s, the emphasis with recorded music was more on sound than on content, and it wasn't unusual for an engineer to call himself a producer, too. They'd take an artist or a band into the studio and use all that wonderful advanced technology to create something with so much ear candy that the listener's attention would be drawn to the sound of the song as much as to the melody and lyrics.

I could never do this. I had three engineers over twenty years who were reliable, compatible, smart, funny, and supportive—and a fourth who was a nightmare. The three good ones allowed me to focus entirely on the music. Over time, my engineer would learn to know what I liked and find ways to make it happen. I could sit in my armchair at the console and ask him to play this or that; as I listened, I'd imagine other instruments or voices joining in, and I'd jot these ideas down and turn them into arrangements—keyboard parts or percussion rhythms or backing vocals or harmonies...

I was free to listen to what was already recorded and to ignore all else. The engineer performing the actual recording operation would dial in the exact sounds I wanted before recording a take. He'd select the microphone, try it out, discover where it needed to be placed in order to capture the instrument most effectively, and then process the sound through a number of remarkable devices to tailor the nature of that sound. There were compressors, limiters, noise gates, delay units, echo chambers, and smaller auxiliary tape decks to provide 'slap-back' or echo; there was a whole section of the recording console devoted to equalizers, which acted as the ultimate bass, midrange, and treble controls. One could select a specific frequency and make anything in that frequency range louder or softer. A dull snare drum could be made to sound snappy with a nice sharp crack on the top, or fatter with a lower midrange boost; the possibilities were endless, and a good engineer knew which tools to use and when to leave well enough alone.

My learning curve was steep but short. I learned what you could do to sound, but not exactly how it was done. I knew what tools were available, but not how they worked. I could listen to a playback, get an idea for a part, explain it to my engineer, and then leave the control room, allowing him to set up for that operation while I preserved my ears and avoided having to sit there during the sometimes arduous process of dialing in the right sound. I didn't want or need to be part of this process, so I'd leave the room and come back in when it was ready to go. This way, I managed to maintain 'fresh ears.' A good engineer was able to sit and focus for hours on end. I have at least a touch of attention deficit disorder, and where the control room is concerned, I was generally up and down, back and forth, in and out.

There were a few technically proficient producers who could engineer and produce at the same time. These folks would begin as engineers and then discover—probably through working with average or poor producers—that they were capable of dealing not with just the sound but with the music as well. (One of my assistant engineers, Neal Avron, worked on many of my sessions during the 1990s, then became a principal engineer/producer and in 2016 was nominated for four Grammys.) I admired these people, but I didn't want to be one of them. For a producer to have a great engineer was a luxury. However good a producer you might be, without the right engineering on a record, it just won't sound that good. Just as good production, good songs, and good musicianship are essential to making a hit, so is good, creative engineering.

When we were at the Sound Pit studio in Atlanta with Ted Nugent, we were told that it was near enough to the CBS studio in Nashville to require a CBS union engineer at our session, even though we were using Tony Reale, a non-union independent engineer from Atlanta. While we toiled away in the control room, the CBS engineer would sit in the lobby, read the newspaper, and collect his hourly salary. When we mixed 'Stranglehold,' I recruited him to pan the backward cymbal from extreme right to extreme left and back. This freed up one of us to handle other mix moves. There were no computerized recording consoles then, so sometimes there would be four or five individuals, each assigned multiple moves on the console. A mix could take on the appearance of a football play.

A good studio will also have some very competent and creative techs—the guys in the shop who fix things and keep all the equipment running well. These are frequently the most colorful people in the recording complex—zany nerds who are stunningly proficient with technology, and who have a top-to-bottom knowledge of electronics.

LAYING IT DOWN: Once we had a good drum performance and the song's foundation was solid, we'd start building the song like a pyramid. Sometimes we'd splice together several sections from different takes of the entire drum performance to avoid errors or inconsistencies. Cutting and splicing a two-inch master tape on a twenty-four-track recording deck is more harrowing than editing on a quarter-inch splicing block in your office.

The occasional audible human error could make a track sound 'live,' in contrast to the repetitive perfection of today's computerized drum tracks. But if you allow a few mistakes to remain uncorrected each time you record a different instrument or vocal, by the time you reach the top of the musical pyramid (usually the lead vocal or percussion), your song will be riddled with little mistakes—and I've never subscribed to the old control-room quip, 'We'll fix it in the mix.' As Harry Belafonte sings in 'Hosanna,' 'House built on a weak foundation will not stand, oh no.'

We'd record the bass guitar over the drum track, and the rhythm guitars over that, and then a 'dummy' (temporary) vocal, keyboards, and whatever else I felt would strengthen or enhance the song. I used instruments like cellos, whole string sections, bagpipes, electric sitar, cardboard boxes, and even a two-by-four wooden plank that I slammed on the floor on Cheap Trick's 'Gonna Raise Hell.' Today, engineers can use a computer to generate any of these sounds and thousands more, but for me, it was more fun to do it organically.

Toward the end of the pyramid-building process, we'd record the lead guitar and keyboards. A dummy vocal was important to have before we recorded the lead guitar, so the guitar player could stay out of the vocalist's way while performing his lead break or solo. Most of the bands I produced didn't have a keyboard player, so I'd hire one after the band finished their parts, and I'd hum the parts I'd like him to play. A band might hire a keyboard player to supply those parts from offstage during their live performances. I loved adding keyboard parts to a recording; they colored the song and created different moods.

The lead vocal and percussion came last. Often, during the mixing process, I'd develop ideas for hand percussion (tambourine, maracas, handclaps, claves, guiros, and so on) and perform all of it (except for congas) myself.

When it came to vocals, I'd print out the lyrics line by line and make three columns next to the lyrics—one for each of the three tracks.

I'd have the singer record three separate performances and then tell him to take fifteen minutes off. The engineer and I would then go through the song line by line, evaluating each of the three performances and combining the best sections of each of the three tracks into one single (fourth) composite vocal track. At that point, I'd have the singer sing two more tracks, and make a second improved composite track.

After that, I'd tell the singer what needed fixing, and we'd re-record just those sections. This could be a whole line or just one word. If the singer was capable, together we could create a solid vocal performance by having him sing just five complete performances and a few inserts. This way, he wouldn't destroy his voice or get bored from repetition.

Before the late 1980s, most producers and artists strived for perfection in tuning, timing, and performance. This was something that rendered me obsolete when Nirvana and the Seattle sound arrived. With the coming of grunge music, perfection began to be equated with sterility, technical artifice, and a 'corporate' approach to rock'n'roll. The musical focus shifted to an infinitely more casual approach, with all those imperfections left in. In fact, many acts valued and strove for imperfection.

MIXING: Mixing a record is like replaying an instrument that's already been played. The band is the instrument, and the mixer plays it. The better the arrangement and performance, the easier the mix. You don't want to go into the mixing stage of a project unless you're totally satisfied with all of your recorded tracks.

Seal's 'Crazy,' Billy Idol's 'Don't Need A Gun,' and Gerry Rafferty's 'Baker Steet' are a few examples of songs that are very well produced and mixed. You can hear every single thing in each song from start to finish. When I was mixing, occasionally I'd try to fit too many instruments into one span of the frequency range—known as 'midrange buildup'—

so I'd have to sacrifice the volume of one instrument to make the others more audible. But in the above three songs, nothing interferes with anything else.

When I started as a producer, the mixing process was completely manual. About fifteen years after I began producing records, the whole mixing process became computerized; when you moved the individual faders up and down to control the volume of each track, the computer remembered those moves and reproduced them with each subsequent playback. You could sit and watch twenty-four faders move by themselves as the song played from top to bottom, and in the earliest computerized consoles, the faders were actually moved by miniature chain drives.

Most producers seem to get a nice balance between the instruments and the vocals, and then they hardly change the sound level of each track from the beginning of the song to the last note. I consciously avoided this kind of 'yardstick' mix, where all the faders would typically be in a straight line across the console. A good level is determined for all the different tracks, and then the mix is pretty much left alone.

When I started producing, the standard multitrack tape machine used tape that was two inches wide. This tape would run across twenty-four separate recording heads, each one a twelfth of an inch in width. When the tracks were full and the recording was complete, the engineer would mix all these tracks together and combine them down to a final two (stereophonic) tracks, with instruments placed from extreme right to extreme left. This process is by far the most complicated and challenging part of any recording project.

Assigning a particular track to both extreme left and extreme right would allow the listener to hear it as if it were coming from the middle. Stereo mixing improved the listening experience vastly. The audio improvement of stereo over mono was as significant as the video improvement of color TV over black-and-white. Conventional mixing almost always presents the drum set as you would see it in a live performance—the kick drum and snare in the middle, the tom-toms and cymbals spread out to the sides.

Before this became the norm, The Beatles experimented with various panning approaches, sometimes assigning the entire drum kit to one side of the stereo mix, for example. On 'Taxman,' from *Revolver*, all the instruments start in the left speaker and all the vocals in the right—then, on the right, a tambourine, followed by a cowbell and George's guitar solo. It was a fascinating experiment. You don't hear that kind of thing anymore.

A&M Studios in LA had an old GM automobile parked right out back. It had an AM radio with a single mono speaker, which was standard factory equipment in the 50s. The studio had equipped the car with a cassette deck, so you could hear how your song sounded in mono.

There are certain features or sections of songs that grab your attention—and I would quite audibly raise their volume in my mix so they would grab the listener's attention. During the 'Cat Scratch Fever' mix, I manually goosed every other three-note guitar runup before the chorus lyric because the notes mirror the vocal line, '*She give me (cat scratch fever).*'

Today this kind of volume change almost never occurs, but some things simply deserve to be pushed up to front and center, like the classic guitar duet between Joe Walsh and Don Felder in 'Hotel California,' or Roger Daltrey's scream in 'Won't Get Fooled Again,' or Keith's intro guitar at the beginning of 'Street Fighting Man' (which sounds like orchestral chimes and is said to have been recorded on a cassette player in his bedroom, like the signature guitar lick in 'Satisfaction'), or the section of that same song that's the closest thing to a bass solo that Bill Wyman ever played with the Stones.

Sometimes a band's A&R man or another label executive would

come to visit the studio and ask to hear the work in progress. Some of them saw themselves as production pros and would suggest that this or that should be louder or softer, so we would be ready with a fader to which no instrument was assigned; this was the 'dummy' fader. When the label person said, 'Maybe that guitar solo should come up a little,' I'd reach over and push the dummy fader up a touch, and we'd play the song again. He'd nod and say that it sounded better, when in fact we hadn't changed a thing. Deceptive, but effective.

After mixing, the producer—usually with some input from the band—puts the songs in the right sequence for the album. I put the two strongest cuts first and second on side one, and the third strongest song as the first cut on side two. The weakest song on the album was reserved for what I called 'the turkey slot'—the next to last track on side two—because I didn't want the weakest song on the record to be the last thing the listener heard.

I always had a band member approve every final mix—either at the studio or via cassette on the road. This way, I couldn't be blamed down the road for not getting it right. Even though this approval by the band was designed to be a safeguard, it frequently failed to do the trick. Despite the fact that every band approved all of my mixes, even forty years later, many of them manage to find all kinds of problems with my performance on their multi-platinum albums.

MASTERING AND DELIVERY: Someone in the band wrote a song and presented it to the other band members, who arranged it and developed individual parts that worked together. Then they recorded it and presented it to the producer on a demo cassette. Like a book editor who takes the author's writing and massages it into a final text, the producer is responsible for taking the unfinished music, developing it, massaging it, and helping to bring it all the way home.

The last chance to massage the sound of the record comes in the mastering lab, where a skilled engineer would cut—or carve—the master disc on a lathe. This disc would be sent to the plant, to be used in the process for pressing into vinyl albums.

Like the recording engineer, the mastering engineer can increase or decrease the level of any single frequency, or perhaps put the whole mix through a compressor, which limits the volume of the loudest sounds and increases the volume of the softest sounds, hopefully enabling each instrument to be easily audible in the mix. This is the final phase of any album project, and for me, it was always the most enjoyable one, because it meant both the completion of the project and a trip back to New York.

I always mastered my records at Sterling Sound, and almost always with mastering engineer George Marino. George could do just about anything I asked for, and the sonic difference between the tape I brought in and the copy I left the building with was remarkable, like the 1970s TV ad for floor wax depicting a layer of sludge being peeled off a kitchen's grimy linoleum floor to reveal a sparkling, brilliant surface underneath.

George would run off a few cassettes of the finished product, and I'd walk them over to the act's label and deliver them to the president and the head of A&R. As of that moment, the recording was in their hands, and I walked out of that building on my way to the next project, feeling like the casino croupier who finishes his shift, claps his hands once, and walks away from the blackjack table.

* * *

After I reached a certain point in my career, I was able to demand contractual provisions other than production fees and royalty rates. I'd often be up against a delivery deadline, and there would be some long days and nights toward the end of the album project. When you're sleep-deprived and exhausted, one of the last things you want to do is drive to LAX, park in the long-term lot, fly coach class to JFK, and cab into Manhattan. It's a long and uncomfortable day, and not ideal to go to the mastering lab to work on a critical phase of an album project while you're fighting the desire to curl up on the mastering studio couch and take a nap.

Once I had achieved success as a producer, though, I had earned the privilege of including a few perks in the album budget, and at the end of a project, I'd enjoy first-class travel from my house to the hotel. When the pilot had turned off the seatbelt sign on the flight from Los Angeles, I'd ask the flight attendant to bring me a bottle of chilled white wine upstairs in the horseshoe-shaped first-class lounge. I'd stay in the lounge for most of the flight, listening to the album on my Walkman and taking notes on the adjustments I wanted to make in the mastering lab the next day. Once in a while, there would be a famous face or two on these flights. Norman Lear once came over to me and asked what I was listening to; we had a nice chat, and I described the mastering process to him. Another time, I sat in on a card game with Mickey Rudin, Sinatra's lawyer.

Once we landed, I would be met at the gate by a limo driver who took my luggage to the car and drove me into Manhattan, where I checked in at the Park Lane Hotel on Central Park South. I'd get settled in the room and then walk over to the Carnegie Delicatessen on 7th Avenue to get a sandwich. This became a ritual.

I would usually stay in the city for a couple of additional nights so I could visit friends, some of whom were still at Epic Records. On the return trip to JFK, I'd stop at a little Danish gourmet deli on the Lower East Side called Old Denmark and pick up an assortment of fabulous spreads, salads, and hors d'oeuvres. The flight attendant would keep these chilled in the galley during the flight, and Suky and I would have friends over for dinner and drinks when I arrived home. This was a really pleasant way to end a project, and I looked forward to it right from the very first day of recording.

Each of my records started to sound a little better than the previous one, but as I made more and more albums, I found that I was becoming pigeonholed. I didn't choose to make hard rock or 'heavy metal' albums—the A&R community just assumed that since I had made this one kind of recording well, it was my specialty, so they continued to give me only more of the same. I'd try to secure a different kind of project, but the 'creative people' who matched artists with producers just weren't able to make that stretch. The simple fact, though, is that making a hit record with Twisted Sister or Mötley Crüe was far more challenging than making a hit record with the Eagles.

Mötley Crüe eventually matured into a professional rock'n'roll band, but sometimes it was an effort just to get them into the studio or to separate a couple of them from their drugs of choice. With an Eagles album, by contrast, a producer could just about sleep on the control room couch for most of the project; they were serious, focused, talented, and motivated, and they could easily have produced their own hit albums if they wanted to.

CHAPTER SIXTEEN

THE STIFFS

The favored term for a record that failed was a 'stiff'—as in dead body. In the 70s, if an act had the support and belief of a record label, they might get away with one or even two stiff album releases before the label reluctantly or impatiently pulled the plug. Things began to change in the 90s. If your debut album was a stiff, you had a good chance of being dropped from the roster. No longer was each album considered to be a rung in the ladder to the top of the charts; an album that followed a stiff could be a waste of money because the act simply wasn't as commercially potent as the label had thought. Today, if your first release isn't a hit, the stringent economics and more corporate nature of the industry require the label to take a closer look at any decision to go forward with the act.

Springsteen's first two albums didn't go above #50 on the Hot 100 chart, but his third, 1975's *Born To Run*, achieved the #3 position. But even if that one had stiffed too, there was a good chance that Columbia Records would have permitted him to make a fourth album, because there was so much passion and support for him at the label. The name of that game was 'artist development,' and major record labels had whole departments devoted to that function. If an act was considered exceptional by the creative people at the label, that act could earn the right to continue making albums until the label learned how to deliver a hit. The awarding of a third or fourth chance was an admission by the label that it took a long time to learn how to properly market an artist—an enlightened attitude for the time.

Every A&R man signs a few stiffs. In order to have a hit, all the stars need to line up—great musicianship, a unique look, a unique sound, a powerful live performance, good songs, and effective promotion, marketing, and distribution. If one of these building blocks is absent or weak, an album could be doomed.

My first disappointment—and my second signing, after REO—was a trio named Robey, Falk & Bod (two last names and a first), whom I considered—and still consider—a brilliant pop trio. The label thought their acoustic guitar and three-part vocal harmony approach was too similar to CSNY, so Epic dropped the band after the first album. I oversaw the album, but I was new to the studio; I wasn't the 'line producer,' and I didn't know that much about how to make a good record. I also didn't have the authority or confidence to convince the label executives at Epic that they were wrong and that the band deserved another shot. Shortly after that, the group America had a huge hit with totally derivative CSNY harmonies. I was pissed. I also felt some responsibility for the fact that my guys had dedicated their lives to their music, and now the company and I had let them down in a big way.

There was a Boston outfit called Orchestra Luna—a combination of straight and openly gay poets and musicians who were easily ten years ahead of their time. Their material made R.E.M. sound conventional. They cracked the live scene at some of the progressive, alternative clubs like CBGB and Max's Kansas City, but the mass commercial appeal just wasn't there. They were brilliant in their own way—fresh, original, inventive—but they were too early for the more alternative college music scene that flourished a decade later.

CBS Records had a winter meeting in Atlanta in 1975, and one night Gregg Geller and I went over to the biggest music club in Atlanta, Alex Cooley's Electric Ballroom. We had no idea who was there that night, but walked in just in time to see this colorfully dressed band incinerate the stage. There were four black and two white musicians playing what can only be described as funky Zeppelin—very hard rock with a major R&B groove. Their name was Mother's Finest, and their live dynamics were stunning. They were fronted by a beautiful petite woman, Joyce Kennedy, who was a superb vocalist—she did it all, and she did it all very well.

This was years before Living Colour, an African American hard rock band that achieved significant success on the rock charts, and who may well have owed a good deal of that success to Mother's Finest. This band was so good that after the show I stood up, looked around, and couldn't understand why there weren't any other A&R people there. With bands this good, I'd expect a bidding war, or at the very least some interest from other labels—but nobody else had shown any interest in them. I didn't have a single doubt about them.

Check out the band's remake of 'Mickey's Monkey' from the album *Another Mother Further* on YouTube. No one was making music like this at that time. They opened for The Who several times, which afforded me the opportunity to meet my biggest musical influence, Pete Townshend—a major moment for me.

Mother's Finest enjoyed a strong cult following, but they never achieved anything near what I thought they should have achieved in terms of fame or record sales. At the weekly staff meeting at Epic in New York, the head of marketing offered that the band lacked airplay because their music was 'too black for white radio and too white for black radio,' so they unfortunately 'fell between the cracks'—a pretty lame evaluation of a weak and ineffective promotional effort on the label's part. Yes, I blame this one on the label.

* * *

In 1978, I was fortunate enough to produce an album for Brownsville Station (best known for 'Smokin' In The Boys' Room') called *Air Special*. Engineer Gary Ladinsky and I made the record in the basement of their manager's office building in Ann Arbor, Michigan. Two Record Plant employees drove the remote studio truck from LA to Michigan, and we stationed it just outside the building's cellar door. The project was a pleasure for me, and there were a few standout tracks, including a cover of Bo Diddley's 'Who Do You Love?,' 'Cooda Crawlin',' and 'Down The Road Apiece.'

This last track was a cover of the Stones' version of a song from the 1940s by Don Raye. I had also recorded another Stones song, 'It's All Over Now,' with Molly Hatchet around the same time. In both cases, the guitar players nailed it, delivering the kind of lead playing that even Keith Richards would have envied. Don't get me wrong—I love Keith's attitude, style, and especially the wonderful riffs he created, but a great technician he was not. Just listen to Brownsville guitarist Cub Koda's performance on this song and you'll see what I mean.

'Who Do You Love?' has been recorded by numerous artists since Bo Diddley cut the original. George Thorogood's version was the biggest hit, but Brownsville's version remains my favorite. It combines a Bo Diddley beat, Chuck Berry-style guitar, and some churning power chords in the double-time final thirty seconds.

In the late 70s, my good friend and CBS Records colleague Gregg Geller—who as an A&R man signed not only Elvis Costello to Columbia but also Labelle to Epic—found another great band from a tiny town called Otho in the middle of Iowa. Otho is actually a *suburb* of Fort Dodge, which itself was a city of only twenty-five thousand people about a hundred miles north of Des Moines. The band was called Hawks, and one of them had somehow managed to get famed recording studio designer Vincent Van Hoff to convert his family's soybean farm chicken coop into a world-class studio.

We made *Hawks* there amid hundreds of acres of soybean fields; when we took a break from recording, we'd hop on an ancient motorcycle and see who could circle the barn the greatest number of times in one minute. Hawks wrote very catchy pop songs with good lyrics, and they sounded just enough like The Beatles to be commercial, but without drawing too obvious a comparison. Once again, though, the album failed to get the attention I thought it so richly deserved.

The hip area called Buckhead was just a ten-minute ride from the Sound Pit in Atlanta. Buckhead, like many artsy, big-city neighborhoods, has long since been gentrified. In the late 70s, there were several good music clubs there. One of these was in a building that had previously been a residence. The ground-floor living area had been converted to a showroom with a small stage, and the club's office was upstairs. I remember the office as well as the stage area because every time we went to this club, which we did frequently after the studio, we were invited upstairs by the generous and affable owner to share in a variety of controlled substances.

It was at this club in 1981 that I first saw a local band called Whiteface, featuring a very talented singer/bass player/songwriter named Kyle Henderson. Whiteface had signed to Mercury Records and made one album that enjoyed minimal success. Shortly after that, Kyle and three other musicians formed a band called The Producers. I liked Kyle very much, both as a musician and a person. He had boundless energy and was cheerful, funny, clever, and optimistic. He was also a great musician and songwriter—a really talented guy.

I went to see this new band, The Producers, and they knocked me right out. As far as I was concerned, they were a home run. They were great musicians, their look and sound were original, and their songs were very infectious. Their music was reminiscent of The Police, but still distinctive. I signed them right away, but the label head wanted them on a new CBS subsidiary label called Portrait, whose records would be distributed by Epic.

The Producers' songs were beyond commercial—you simply couldn't get them out of your head. Like Mother's Finest, they were unusual, unique, edgy, and visually appealing. I was delighted with them. A couple of their singles made the charts, but after two LPs, *The Producers* and *You Make The Heat*, the label dropped them. As far as I was concerned, though, they were superb writers and performers, and whatever was lacking in my production was more than made up for by their songs and musicianship. 'What's He Got?' from the first LP felt like an undeniable hit, pure and simple, and I'll never understand how it could have been ignored by radio, even with the dreadful single edit (I didn't do it). Check it out, and then try 'She Sheila' and 'Dear John.'

I felt terrible for that band. I had brought them to the label and produced their records, and they had only a modestly successful run, instead of the huge impact I had envisioned.

During my twelve years with Epic, I produced twenty albums. Of course, not every one of the bands I signed would make it to the top, but when they didn't, I felt disappointed that I'd failed to deliver the success I was positive they all deserved. I've never doubted that I was right to expect this success, or that they were all hugely talented. You can't win 'em all, but in the case of these bands, I sure believed I could.

* * *

One day I got a call from Paul Cooper, head of the West Coast Atlantic Records office, asking me if I might be interested in producing The Blues Brothers' second album. I was a huge fan of *Saturday Night Live*, and I was jazzed by the prospect of working in the studio with Aykroyd and Belushi.

I told Paul I'd be interested in exploring the idea, and he suggested bringing John and Judy Belushi over to our house for dinner. This was exciting news—not so much for the music, but for a chance to spend time with John, who was arguably the most famous and charismatic entertainer in the country at the time. I loved him. Everyone in my generation loved him. *SNL* was huge, *Animal House* was legendary, and I was thrilled to have him at our home.

We made a date. Our house was on Laurel Hills Road, a narrow cul-de-sac off Laurel Canyon Boulevard. There was barely room for two cars to pass one another on the street, and while our neighbors were accustomed to seeing an occasional Lincoln Town Car take me to and from the airport, the arrival of a big black stretch limo with tinted windows aroused some curiosity on our quiet suburban street. John, Judy, Paul Cooper, and Smokey, John's assistant and driver, came inside, and we had a few drinks in the living room. John was monkeying around with our daughter, Nina, who was about four at the time, and managed to drop her over the back of the living room couch onto the floor. Fortunately, she was a good sport, and we had a thick living room rug. John seemed not to notice.

John was the most hyperactive person I had ever met. He was unable to sit still. To borrow from *Spinal Tap*, he was on '11' all the time, and to say he had a severe case of attention deficit disorder was just the beginning. Still, it made him who he was, and it worked for him.

During dinner, we discussed songs that might be appropriate for the album, and John mentioned that part of Smokey's job description was to 'take the cocaine out of my nose.' Being with John reinforced my feeling that the more eccentric you were, the more people admired you—maybe for your courage, maybe for your confident air of independence. So many successful LA individuals behaved in such an unusual manner. I'm pretty conventional, and it was something of an effort for me to relate to John in a way that I felt was effective, or that would convince him that I was a good choice for the job.

After dinner, we moved to what was then called our media room, and John went through my album collection, picking out songs that he liked and that he might want to record for the album. He danced around the room with total abandon, grabbing my sister Martha, who was happy to be dancing with this frenetic man. (She had recently returned from fifteen years in Denmark and had no idea who he was.)

In March of 1981, I went up to the Blues Brothers office in Manhattan to discuss the project in greater detail with John and Dan. The driver's side door from a Chicago Police cruiser leaned against the office wall. John was a no-show, so I sat with Dan for a while and discussed our plans for an album. Despite inhaling a copious amount of weed, Dan was serious, articulate, and focused.

Because John couldn't make it to the meeting, we arranged to spend a little time together in New York. I arrived at his apartment downtown, spent a few minutes with him and Judy, and then he and I departed for JP's, a club on the Upper East Side where I sometimes went to evaluate bands. I followed John across the club floor to a stairway in the back. Upstairs was a small warren of rooms that most likely served as owner Jimmy Pullis's office and home. People were talking and drinking. As soon as John spied the first lines of cocaine on a coffee table, he grabbed me, and in a flash we were back on the sidewalk. To his credit, he just didn't want to hack it, so we went back downtown to a large restaurant venue I'd never seen before. The main room in the restaurant was huge—there must have been almost a hundred people in there having a good old time, laughing, talking loudly, eating, and drinking.

John pushed open the door and we paused just inside, taking in the busy late-evening scene. In seconds, the noise in the room fell to a murmur, and everybody turned their heads. Just about every single person in the room was staring at John—and although I was standing there right next to him, I promptly became invisible.

So this is what real fame looks like, I remember thinking to myself.

After a surprisingly clean and sober night of Manhattan club-hopping, I bailed at around 2am while John took off for some other after-hours spot. I don't know if he made it through the night drug-free, but he certainly did his best while he was with me. To be honest, I was a little disappointed to find that he was on the wagon, as I'd been looking forward to partying with him. That's just the way we were back then. But I relished the few hours I spent with this fascinating man, even though he remained as enigmatic at the end of the night as he was at the beginning.

The next morning, as I reflected on the few hours we spent together aimlessly hopping around from this bar to that club, never alighting at any one spot for more than a few minutes, I realized that while he kept me and many others entertained for the whole time, I couldn't recall him smiling once.

Ultimately, I passed on doing the album—partly because there was no new movie to support it, and partly because I thought it would be pretty difficult to get the right quality of musical performances out of Dan and John. I was too familiar with the behavior of out-of-control, self-destructive musicians in the studio, and from what I understood about his behavior during the making of the first movie, he made Mötley Crüe look diligent and cooperative. Nevertheless, I felt fortunate to have known him, albeit briefly, and I was very sorry to see him go. He was one of a kind.

SIDE D
BURNING HOT

CHAPTER SEVENTEEN

ELEKTRA: A ROADBLOCK AND A PRODUCTION DEAL

When I first came to work at Epic in New York, I was happy to be making $10,000 a year. Twelve years later, after signing five bands to Epic that had sold a combined forty million albums, my salary was considerably higher, but in my opinion still modest. I had an office and shared a secretary, but I was spending all my time in the recording studio producing records. Many of these were very successful. As my Epic contract was due to run out in 1982, I went in to see Dick Asher, who was then president of CBS Records and happened to be visiting the West Coast offices. I asked him for a raise.

'Tom,' he replied, 'it just isn't the same record business anymore.' He declined to grant me the raise I had requested.

I liked Dick very much, but I told him that I thought I was worth much more than I was making, since I had signed five huge acts and produced eleven gold and platinum records for Epic. And, I added, if I didn't get the raise, I'd have to look for another label.

That was the last I heard from Dick, so in the spring of 1982, I reluctantly departed Epic Records. I don't think there was another job in the world that could have been more enjoyable or exciting than the one I had there. What a time it was.

When I left CBS, there were articles in the trade papers (*Variety, Billboard, Record World*) about my exit, and one of the people who noticed was Joe Smith, the head of Elektra Records.

Following a visit to his Beverly Hills home and lunch at the wonderful Hillcrest Country Club, Joe hired me as Elektra's vice president of

A&R, tasked with helping to revitalize the label's tired roster. My visit to his home reminded me of a visit I had made a few years earlier to Mo Ostin's house for a lunch meeting and an invitation to come to Warner Bros Records as a staff producer. Joe had also headed up Warners, but only days after I signed my contract, my old friend and mentor Bruce Lundvall—head of Elektra's New York office and the number two man at the label—informed me that Joe was being kicked upstairs.

Joe's replacement would be Bob Krasnow, a successful A&R executive at Warner Bros. Shortly after I began working with Bob, it became apparent that I wouldn't be able to maintain any real independence in my position. Even though Bob chose to keep me on and honor my contract, it was clear that he considered himself the actual head of A&R.

During his first week on the job, Bob asked me and my A&R assistant, Tom Zutaut, to lunch and told us that his first move would be to drop Mötley Crüe from the artist roster because he felt they were 'an embarrassment to the label.' In the politest terms I could manage, I replied that while I respected Bob's preference for accomplished but less commercial artists, hard rock was a very profitable genre, and someone had to pay the label's bills.

Fortunately, *Shout At The Devil* would soon explode, so by then it was too late for Bob to drop the band. I think he learned something from this experience, as he later allowed Elektra A&R man Michael Alago to sign Metallica to the label.

Bob soon brought in producer Roy Thomas Baker as an A&R consultant, which effectively marginalized my position. The writing was on the wall; it seemed like Bob had little respect for my musical choices or direction.

During my brief stint at Elektra, I had meetings with David Lindley, Ms. Ellas McDaniel (wife of Bo Diddley), and The Cars; I even had lunch with Judy Collins at her favorite New York restaurant. Irving Azoff called, asking me to find out how Eagles bass player Timothy B. Schmitt was doing with the solo album he was working on at home. I called Mr. Schmitt three times, but he blew me off each time; I think he'd had his fill of label guys. I was disappointed by this because I had met him in my early days at Epic, when he was a member of Poco, but since he didn't know me he probably assumed I was just another label 'suit' who didn't know much about music.

When I departed Elektra, I agreed to a deal to produce three albums for the label with an up-front contractual payment, which paid my family's expenses for the next year. One of those albums would be *Shout At The Devil*, which would soon establish me within a small group of solid hard-rock producers.

* * *

During my brief time at Elektra, I attended a meeting with the New York staff, where my old friend and mentor, former CBS Records president Bruce Lundvall—now VP of the label—invited me to join him for an artist's showcase. We cabbed downtown to a small rehearsal studio where a beautiful African American girl of nineteen sang her heart out for us and a few other people—mostly friends and family. Bruce had seen her perform once previously and knew her manager. I was grateful to him for respecting my position as head of A&R, and for seeking my opinion.

The girl performed a brief, brilliant set with a backing band of professional musicians, singing what I'd say were gospel-flavored middle-of-the-road songs—not really R&B. Her voice was powerful, and she sang with urgency, intensity, and joy—she was phenomenal. When she finished, Bruce and I looked at each other, and I just laughed. I didn't have to say anything—she was that good.

We spoke with her and her manager for a few minutes. She was sparkling and gracious—a very attractive young lady in all respects. We thanked them and returned to the midtown Elektra office, where we excitedly described her to Krasnow. I was delighted to share a role in discovering an artist this good, and I never would have known about her without Bruce inviting me along.

'Urban' music had been Krasnow's specialty at Warner Bros, and now, at our insistence, he went to see this girl perform. It was reported to me later that Bob's response was, 'Why should I sign someone who sounds like Chaka Khan when I just signed Chaka Khan [at Warner]?'

And that's how the young Whitney Houston got away.

A few months later, ex-CBS promotion man Gerry Griffith took Clive Davis (who had established the new Arista Records) to see Whitney perform, and you know the rest. As Whitney's career exploded and the months went by, I was told that Krasnow placed the blame for his blunder on Bruce—but that's one of the risks you take if you want a career in showbiz. It comes with the territory.

CHAPTER EIGHTEEN

MÖTLEY CRÜE: ORGANIZED CHAOS

Mötley Crüe were four savvy and intelligent guys whose priorities were very different from mine. They didn't merely have a disregard for convention—they despised it. Their bad behavior is legendary—and not at all exaggerated—but I honestly didn't see too much of it in the recording studio. They did most of their serious partying after the session or away from the studio, and much of the *real* debauchery had probably occurred a couple of years before I met them, when they were playing clubs on the Sunset Strip and all living together in what they described as a hellhole of an apartment.

Our recording sessions didn't devolve into orgies; we managed to accomplish things at a reasonable pace. I didn't party with them, primarily because their kind of fun was too hardcore for me. I was about fifteen years older than they were, and many of their drugs of choice went beyond the category of 'party favors.' I was also never actually invited. But I wasn't so detached from them that I didn't enjoy the association—I did. In spending lots of time with them, I had gone from hanging with obedient and sheltered folks as a young man to hanging with just-short-of-criminals as an adult.

Here I was, a conventional Ivy League preppie who had grown up in a pretty formal environment, consorting with rebellious, irreverent, rude, and potentially dangerous guys. I got a kick from being connected to people like that, without having to behave the way they did. It was as if I was a temporary and protected member of a well-behaved biker gang.

I was introduced to the Crüe by Tom Zutaut, who signed them after they built a healthy LA following to the point where they could create a line around the block at Sunset Strip clubs like the Whiskey, the Roxy, or Gazzarri's. Tom thought I was the right guy to produce them, and he convinced me to consider taking them on. The band's first LP, *Too Fast For Love*, had been recommended to me by my New York friend and Epic colleague Doreen Courtright, but to me, the album was a little sloppy. I was convinced that power in music couldn't be achieved without the proper pitch, a steady meter, and control (precisely what most big new bands would do away with in the 90s).

The band and I met in my Elektra office, and right away they adopted a defensive posture. They had had a bad time with their first manager, and they harbored a general distrust of music industry people. While they knew of my work with Ted Nugent, Cheap Trick, and Molly Hatchet, they knew nothing about me personally. Things were a little tense until Tommy Lee spoke up.

'If this guy wants to produce our album,' he said, 'then maybe we should listen to what he has to say.'

I was grateful for that, and we did eventually agree to work together. But there was never any doubt that I was there as a helper, and not one of the boys.

Bass player Nikki Sixx and drummer Tommy Lee were the two leaders of the band. I don't think that guitarist Mick Mars or front man Vince Neil wanted that kind of responsibility. Vince pretty much wanted to be left alone to party, and Mick, it seemed, simply wanted to be left alone, although he was the one I was closest to in the studio. I had heard from one of their roadies that on the road Mick preferred to stay in his hotel room and draw the shades. It was mainly Nikki who drove the Mötley Crüe train and who was largely responsible for their songs, their image, and their reputation as the bad boys of LA.

Nikki was smart and creative and had a wry sense of humor, but for a while these sharp attributes would be dulled by heroin. I enjoyed the little personal time I spent with him; outside of music, we had little in common, but I was fascinated by his whole 'fuck the world' attitude, which was one largely shared by Tommy and Vince.

Tommy was the band's spark plug. His enthusiasm was boundless, and he was always up for a new adventure—particularly when it had to do with recording, and specifically when it had to do with his drums. He was cheerful, cooperative, and enthusiastic in the studio, and when I think back to those sessions, I remember him smiling most of the time. He seemed delighted to be in the studio. He was generally so positive in his approach to life that he found it hard to say no to anything.

I produced three albums for Mötley Crüe. The first one, *Shout At The Devil*, established the band and put them near the top of the heap. It was also a challenge in several ways. Nikki Sixx had an injured shoulder, and his arm was in a sling, which made playing the bass difficult, so it took several hours to record his parts for each song. By the time I stopped working with the band five years later, however, he had become an accomplished bass player.

Mick Mars, meanwhile, had some nice, well-rehearsed fills and solos ready to go, but his guitar sound was ratty—distorted, but not in a good way. To me, it just sounded as though the speakers in his amp were torn and tired, and it wasn't until *Girls, Girls, Girls* that he found a good guitar tech who really made a difference in the studio. My routine practice of doubling the rhythm guitar parts resulted in a less gnarly sound—something that was effective in getting Mötley Crüe on hit AM radio stations, but also something that the band didn't particularly appreciate.

Since the Crüe were a local band, I decided to have a little wrap party when we finished *Shout At The Devil* in order to thank them and to celebrate what I considered a successful project. I invited the band, their crew, and their girlfriends to our home in Laurel Canyon, and we had a barbecue by the pool. It was a nice gathering, but no one brought a bathing suit. Tommy would use any excuse to remove his clothes onstage, but here he stayed fully covered.

Instead of behaving in the way we'd grown accustomed to—getting high, stripping down, and doing a cannonball into the pool—the Crüe remained in their black leathers, sitting sweltering by the poolside. Back then, musicians rarely spent time outdoors, and the sunlight gleamed off their pale, tattooed skin.

My wrap party barbecue would become a tradition, and I organized one at the end of every album project I did in LA. While the names and faces of the invited guests changed over the years, one thing remained the same: when rock stars are poolside, they prefer to stay out of the water and sit baking in the hot Southern California sun.

* * *

The second album I produced for Mötley Crüe, *Theater Of Pain*, was an even more challenging project due to the increasing frequency of the band's drug use. I didn't feel the songwriting was up to their potential, and it didn't help that the recording was tightly sandwiched between lengthy tours. This was a common problem. When a band had a big hit with their debut album, they usually needed to go right out on a hastily booked tour to support the record. Then they'd have to go directly into the studio when they came off the road, and because their agent had booked the next big tour for them based on their recent success, they needed to grind out a follow-up album in a limited amount of time. This would prove stressful, and would often lead to both fewer strong songs and increased drug use.

A few rock critics and some of the bands I worked with over the years felt that my musical approach was too refined, too 'pop,' and they had a point; I was a pop guy, not a metalhead. But I think this helped the Crüe to become successful. I could assist in rearranging the songs, get rid of the fat, and keep the meat. This was an effective way to produce a hit single. Their music, as it was presented to me, wasn't appropriate for AM radio at the time, but as I did with all bands, I tried to take the best parts of each song and highlight them while downplaying or simply eliminating the not-so-interesting parts.

The third album I made with the band, *Girls, Girls, Girls*, provided a hit single of the same name that went to #12 on the *Billboard* pop charts. By the time we got to that record, the band's sound—particularly Mick's guitar sound—had changed. I liked the change, but I think the band would have preferred something dirtier. Fortunately for me, they were usually too busy or too distracted to address that particular issue.

Occasionally, I'd go out with the band to different clubs in town. I went on tour with them for a couple of days, shared memorable moments with them in the studio, attended Vince's and Tommy's bachelor parties and wedding parties, and (as mentioned earlier) even accepted an invitation from Nikki to meet him for sushi just hours after he had been officially pronounced dead.

Tommy's romance with Heather Locklear was a bit of a mystery to me. Heather was well bred, well educated, refined, and came from an upscale LA suburb. Tommy was a wonderful guy, but he was clearly from the wrong side of the tracks. Maybe that was what Heather found attractive. She clearly had a thing for musicians, as she would later marry Bon Jovi guitarist Richie Sambora. I liked Heather very much; she was level-headed, friendly, and accessible. When she and Tommy attended an event together, she'd occasionally wait patiently in the limo while Tommy did his thing inside.

Tommy and Heather were married in Santa Barbara at the Biltmore (now the Four Seasons), a lovely upscale hotel right on the water. It was a beautiful, refined affair, probably in great part as a result of Heather's involvement. Even so, given the nature of the guests on the groom's side of the aisle, it's fair to say that refreshments other than alcohol were in abundance.

Vince's engagement party was held at the Tropicana, a mud-wrestling club downtown, just off the Hollywood Freeway. I brought along a friend who was visiting us from the east, to show him another side of Hollywood. Vince was marrying a girl who worked there—not as a wrestler but as a numbers girl. Her name was Sharise, and she was the one who would walk around the ring in some fetching apparel, holding a sign high in the air with the number of the next round on it. My friend Bud and I sat down in the front row next to the mud pit, and some of the wrestlers came out to mix and mingle; since I was a transplanted uptight Boston boy, I moved to the second row; for better or worse, my starchy New England breeding discouraged me from getting too close to these girls.

Vince's wedding to Sharise was a fine affair, held at the upscale Bel Air Hotel. Suky and I were surprised to discover that Vince had a young adult son who introduced himself as Jason. We were seated at the same table, and he told us that he was preparing to go to law school. He looked like any boy of his age, neither tattooed nor inappropriately dressed, nor sporting long hair, and after the wedding Suky and I expressed our surprise to one another, concluding that Jason, compared to Vince, may have been from another universe.

* * *

During the years we worked together, there were very few cross words between me and the band, and no apparent bad feelings. Yet when they selected Bob Rock to produce the follow-up to the multi-platinum *Girls, Girls, Girls*, they didn't even invite me to their record-release party, which was held just a few miles from my home.

Bob did a fine job producing the Crüe's fifth album, *Dr. Feelgood*. With every other band I produced, if they switched to another producer, the resulting album sold far less than the most recent one I had done. This was true with Ted Nugent, Molly Hatchet, Cheap Trick, Twisted Sister, Poison, LA Guns, Kix, and so on, but *Dr. Feelgood* was the exception. The band was freshly clean and sober, which greatly improved their musical performance, and I still feel that 'Kickstart My Heart' is probably the best song they ever did.

Doc McGhee and two of his associates, Rich Fisher and Doug Thaler, performed the truly heroic task of managing Mötley Crüe. Doc also managed Jon Bon Jovi, who appeared to me to be a pretty straight-ahead, grounded guy—kind of a rock'n'roll businessman. This was fortunate for Doc and his crew, because Mötley Crüe was more than a handful.

Doc is a smart, savvy, funny guy who I believe was one of the very few managers who would have been able to deal with Mötley's brand of mayhem. He had a way of taking control, introducing you to his unique perspective on things, and calmly laying down the rules—I imagine he could even make you feel better about yourself while he was firing you.

Doc is also a fine golfer. Each winter, the winner of the annual Kelly–Baruck Invitational hosted a smaller three-day tournament. One year after I had finished with the Crüe, Doc won the tournament, so we all convened at his beautiful home south of LA. He threw a nice barbecue around a huge firepit in his big backyard. I arrived a little late, and as I walked down the stairs to the backyard, someone sitting by the fire pit jokingly yelled, 'Ladies and gentlemen, Tom Werman.' Heather Locklear, who was also sitting by the fire pit, jumped up and shouted, 'Tom Werman!?' She ran over and gave me a big hug. I have never seen so many jaws drop at one time.

Some years later, I ran into Vince at a movie premiere. He gave me a big smile and a hug as if I were a close friend; it didn't matter that we hadn't spoken in several years, or that we'd never see each other again. It was nice to see Vince and get a warm hello, but I'll always be curious about the ability of a rock star to ignore you completely for more than a decade, and then greet you like a bosom buddy.

In retrospect, it feels as though a lot of the rock musicians I worked with placed little or no value on our collaboration. Unlike almost everyone I know who's *not* in the entertainment industry, rock musicians seem to have no interest in reconnecting or reminiscing—something I really enjoy doing. If you can no longer be of any specific use to them, you basically cease to exist.

I don't believe they thought there was anything wrong with this; it's fairly common in the LA entertainment industry. While you're instrumental in helping bands to create records that sell millions, you're their buddy—lots of jokes, pats on the back, shared recreational drugs, glasses raised high. Years later, when their careers have peaked, they're able to carefully document how your alleged lack of talent and focus was responsible for just about everything they failed to achieve, both as individuals and as a band.

In 2007, Nikki Sixx published his book *The Heroin Diaries*, which, to my surprise, was reviewed in the prestigious Book Review section of the Sunday *New York Times*. I started reading it with interest, but I was disappointed by his unflattering and flatly inaccurate recollection of how the albums were made, and his portrayal of me as a detached, uninterested, and barely involved slacker. I wrote a letter to the editor contradicting much of what Nikki wrote about our respective roles in the studio. The newspaper published the letter, which led to a protracted verbal battle between Nikki and me. (My response to him should be readily available online, should you care to check it out.)

About ten years later, I was surprised to receive a phone call from Nikki. He sounded personable and was not unfriendly. We chatted for a while, and I said I'd been thinking about going to New York to see them in concert on their farewell tour.

'Come on down,' he said jokingly. 'I know the bass player.'

I followed up by sending an email to him, asking who I should call about getting the tickets. Regrettably, I never heard back. It became apparent that his call was probably just a requirement to 'make amends' in the 12 Step recovery program.

* * *

Back in 1983, shortly after we completed work on *Shout At The Devil*, I took my family to see *This Is Spinal Tap*. I don't mean to draw any specific comparisons here, but having been in close quarters with several hard rock bands by then, I was just about the only person in the theater who wasn't laughing hysterically. I was a little sobered by the movie; I sympathized with the band and was concerned about their future. They didn't see the writing on the wall, and they didn't have a clue that it was over for them. The thought of a band like Mötley Crüe ever losing favor with their fans and drawing a fraction of their 1984 audience was a new and frightening one for me.

About a year after the movie's release, I was invited to a meeting at MCA Records headquarters in Universal City with the *Spinal Tap* cast to discuss the possibility of my producing an as-yet-unnamed album for them. I was delighted to meet and speak with Christopher Guest, Michael McKean, and especially Harry Shearer, who had a fascinating Sunday morning show on National Public Radio.

Christopher was serious, and I felt that it was something of an effort for him to carry on a conversation. Michael McKean was easygoing with a ready smile, and he told me he was a big Cheap Trick fan. Harry was Harry, and I tried to be sharp with him since his intellect and wit were so obvious on his radio show.

There were a few other producer candidates in attendance, including ace guitarist, Toto member, and very nice guy Steve Lukather, who would eventually appear as a guest musician on the follow-up Spinal Tap album, *Break Like The Wind*, some eight years later. There are several producers on that record—accomplished veterans—and a long list of talented and famous guest musicians.

I never heard any more from the band, but it was a great afternoon, and I always felt good when I discovered that an accomplished musician (or actor or producer or singer) even knew my name. I was honored to have been included among the candidates to produce the band. Both *This Is Spinal Tap* and *Animal House* remain the two most-quoted films in the Werman family, and 'This one goes to 11' has been a favorite saying in recording studios since 1984.

CHAPTER NINETEEN

COCAINE (BLINDED BY THE LIGHT)

A couple of weeks after the release of *Shout At The Devil*, I was kicking back in my room at the Pebble Beach Lodge after a round of golf at the Kelly–Baruck Invitational. I got a phone call from Tom Zutaut, and the first thing he said was, 'Werman, we have a hit.' The album was selling like hotcakes and numbers were increasing daily.

The word on the street was out. After we congratulated each other and hung up the phone, I made myself a stiff drink and put out a couple of lines of coke—not to celebrate but to protect myself from the feeling of dread that came over me when I realized I'd have to duplicate or surpass the success of this album when I did the next one. This was the small price I regularly paid for a hit record.

* * *

In 1972, I was on a flight to a Midwest CBS Records sales conference when one of my Epic Records buddies walked forward to my seat and quietly suggested I might want to take his packet of cocaine into the lavatory. My drug experience up to then had been limited to marijuana; despite my college classmates' urging, I had avoided the psychedelics they enjoyed for years (acid, mescaline, mushrooms, psilocybin, and so on), and to me, the ending '–aine' (Lidocaine, Novocaine, Xylocaine) was a no-no. I was a control freak, not inclined to expand my use of illegal substances on an airplane to a company event. So I thanked my CBS buddy and declined.

At the hotel that evening, he came to my room to have a drink before the dinner and show. There he explained that cocaine was not at all psychedelic and that I should try it. He 'just knew' I'd like it. This proved to be a serious understatement.

The list of things he claimed it could do sounded too good to be true, but because of his generosity and enthusiasm, and because of my growing curiosity, I agreed to do a couple of lines. I paced back and forth in the narrow space between the beds and the bureau, nervously waiting for fire-breathing serpents to emerge from the walls. Instead, after a minute or two, I found myself feeling energetic, confident, and pleasantly stress-free. In short, I liked it. I liked it very much. I asked if I could maybe have a little more before we went down to the ballroom.

We both did another couple of lines, and that evening I single-handedly entertained the whole table for the length of the entire meal. The combination of white wine and cocaine produced a buoyant sensation of confidence and energy I hadn't known before; I thought I sounded quite witty, and it's possible that I actually was.

The next day, I asked my friend how I could get some more of this stuff, and he said he'd take care of me when we returned to New York. The rest, as they say, is history. For the next fifteen years, I was rarely without a little reserve of cocaine. I didn't do it every day, but I did feel secure having it around, just in case I *felt* like doing it. For the first few years, the quality didn't matter much; good or not so good, it always worked. As time went by, I could tell the quality instantly by the taste, the sting, or the smell. Just as with weed, the brain adjusts to this stuff over time, and the drug's effects change accordingly. With both cocaine and marijuana, the first few times are the best; no matter how hard or how many times you try, you just can't reproduce those experiences.

In 1982, I was in a suite at the Fairmont Hotel in San Francisco with a label president who graciously offered me some of his personal stash. It was as close to pure as anything I'd ever had—truly a different substance from the one I had come to know. It sparkled like crystalline snow under the night lights. I remember being struck at that moment by how much money I must have thrown away over the years on mediocre blow that was cut with baby laxative or maybe baking soda, while the powder this guy had was probably available from someone, somewhere in LA at only a slightly higher price. That night, what I inhaled didn't affect my appetite, I didn't babble endlessly, my pulse stayed constant—the whole experience was excellent. My focus was sharp, and everything appeared to be quite clear. I decided that if I had access to quality contraband like this, I'd probably do it every day—just as it was rumored my host did.

In the 80s, everyone in LA was doing coke. My recording engineer's wife worked in a medical office, and she told him all the doctors were doing it. Lawyers were doing it. Cops and judges were doing it. If you went to a party, everyone was holding; at one party I attended in Beverly Hills, a little saucer of cocaine sat on the coffee table. It may have cost the host $1,000, but it was *the* party drug—and for those first few years, we all thought it was just a harmless social thing, like weed.

Certain restaurants and clubs catered to the record business, and these places tended to be permissive and relaxed. I recall a time when a woman who was an Epic Records executive was having drinks with one of my A&R colleagues at a Sunset Boulevard spot called Le Dome; they were seated in a side room at a booth, furtively snorting coke off of their fingertips. She accidentally dropped her little dark brown vial of powder, and it rolled under her seat. My friend bent down, reached under the bench, and quickly retrieved it. He took his seat and discreetly handed her the little bottle. She glanced down at it and said, 'This isn't my bottle.' That's how common coke was.

Over the ensuing decade, most of us came to realize that cocaine was, in fact, an evil little substance that created some unfortunate dependencies. When I finally stopped doing it, I had to train myself to be sociable again. I'd grown accustomed to popping into the lavatory next to our front door for a couple of lines before I left the house for a club or a party, and I'd bring some along to do later in the evening. I'd frequently be treated to some at the party (or dinner, or concert) anyway. It wasn't in the nature of the drug to do it alone. It was more fun to get high with someone else—and the more you did, the more generous you became with your stash.

I liked how coke introduced me to my evil twin—the one who would say clever things, do things that I wouldn't normally do, and handle social situations with aplomb and wit. I gleefully departed from my comfort zone.

Night-time recording sessions were fueled by a combination of cheap white wine (Bolla Soave at about three dollars a bottle) and cocaine. It was a potent combination, generating the kind of energy that could in turn generate some good musical creativity. I'd seen other producers use coke at work. One producer whose work I admired very much would put a little saucer of blow on the console, dip the lit end of a cigarette into the powder, and smoke as he normally would. He must have functioned effectively this way since his records were well-produced and very successful.

When our sessions ended, usually around midnight, few of the people who worked at the studio—clients or staff—would say goodnight and immediately depart for home. Most nights, they'd hang out for a while, and 'a while' could sometimes extend to sunrise. People from the record label might drop in, and after a brief hello and a quick playback of what we were working on, they'd repair to the recreational areas of the studio.

There was a jacuzzi room at the Record Plant that could be reserved by clients on an hourly basis. It had a big redwood tub that was sunk into the floor, a sofa, a coffee table with a glass top that was perfect for chopping out lines of coke, a bed, a couch, and a stack of towels. It was designed as a place to refresh oneself, or to unwind after a hard day and night in the studio—but really it was a good party room, and it saw far more activity than passivity.

If this wasn't enough (and in the age of excess, what was enough?), each of the three studios had its own private lounge in the rear of the building; these rooms, with wall-to-wall carpeting, a stereo, a TV, and a couch, were designed as retreats for producers or musicians who desired a break or a nap, or who simply needed to wait until it was their turn to record.

Most nights you would find a few unattached males who'd show up and work their way into the after-hours group in the hope they'd be offered a couple of lines. Sometimes they got lucky. Even luckier were the girls who would show up in pairs, dressed to kill, who mixed, mingled, and flirted. The poor guys with the powder would supply these girls with liberal amounts, hoping to be rewarded at the end of the evening. Over time, these same guys learned that most of the girls were there for the drugs, period. The most notorious of them earned the uncomplimentary title of 'coke whores.' They chatted, they drank, they snorted, and they laughed, but in the end, the guys went home alone. The sad part was that this little tragicomedy would play over again the very next night, and the night after that. Hope does spring eternal.

My stimulant/depressant combination worked so effectively for the creative process that I came to believe it was a requirement in order for me to get my creative juices flowing. When I was lit, the band was lit, and we all became pretty creative and pretty industrious. In a twelve-hour work day, we'd do our best work in just a few evening hours. It wasn't always party time in the control room during evening sessions, but it certainly wasn't always a focused grind. If the band had visitors, we could get sidetracked for a while, but we turned out a reasonable amount of quality rock'n'roll—even under the influence.

I tended to have several weeks off between projects, which was time enough to rid myself of the toxins. (An article in the *British Medical Journal* found that forty years after they attained their initial fame, North American rock stars were only 87 percent as likely to be alive as 'normal people of the same age and ethnicity.' Note that all people other than North American rock stars were described as 'normal people.')

One day, I bought a gram of coke from one of my artists and went into a stall in the bathroom where, with not a little anticipation, I unwrapped the tightly tucked Sno-Seal, then proceeded to drop the whole packet into the toilet. There was nothing I could do about it, so I exited the bathroom, found the supplier, and immediately bought another gram. Seventy-five bucks down the hopper—a lot of money in 1978—but the powder was important to the process, so the high price didn't keep me from making a second purchase.

* * *

Back in 1974, the annual CBS Records convention at the Century Plaza Hotel in LA attracted most of the coke dealers in town. On the day we checked in, there was so much buying and selling that the lobby looked like the trading floor of the Chicago Commodities Exchange. Still new to LA at the time, I was introduced to a fellow who sold me a small amount of what I thought was cocaine. In my room, I laid out a couple of lines before going down to the ballroom for the big dinner show. Cocaine that was cut with another substance (baby laxative?) could provide a slight stinging sensation at the top of the nasal passage, but this stuff produced a sharp, searing pain unlike anything I had ever experienced.

Feeling a little speedy, I had a few drinks at the cocktail reception, and a few more with dinner. After the show, there were parties in the hospitality suites upstairs, and the revelry continued until long after midnight. I finally crawled into bed at about 2:30 in the morning. I couldn't sleep, and after about a half-hour I broke out in a serious sweat and passed out. Only afterward did it occur to me that what I thought was cocaine was actually methamphetamine. Laying in sheets soaked with perspiration and feeling grateful to be alive, I vowed never to make this error again. To this day, I can't understand how people become speed freaks. It's dreadful stuff.

Regrettably, however, cocaine was just what the doctor ordered when it came to self-medication as a cure for anxiety. As my career grew more solid and more successful, I came to rely on coke to avoid feeling insecure. Fear of failure is a common thing, but I developed what amounted to a fear of success. By the time I was familiar with coke as a recreational supplement, I'd made seven platinum albums with three different artists over eight years. I was sought-after and well paid, and the industry had come to expect success from any album I produced. This created increasing pressure with each project, and I was afraid that each one would be the time when I'd be revealed as a lucky impostor who didn't deserve the professional respect that came with these hit albums, and who would tumble from the pedestal, only to spend the rest of his career trying to regain his former level of success.

The producer/engineer Steve Albini once commented, 'In the back of the mind of every engineer I've met, they feel like they don't really know what they're doing. Everybody has this nagging doubt that they're a fraud. You have to get comfortable with that feeling.'

Cocaine helped a lot of music industry professionals get pretty comfortable with that feeling.

CHAPTER **TWENTY**

FIGHTING DOKKEN TOOTH AND NAIL

By the time I got to Elektra, Tom Zutaut, who had brought Mötley Crüe to the label, had also signed a band named Dokken. I was not familiar with the band, but since *Shout At The Devil* had become such a big hit, 'Zute' was sure that I would be the right producer for Dokken. I was agreeable too, because it would be the second part of the three-album production deal I'd signed when I left the label.

Frontman Don Dokken and guitarist George Lynch did not get along; in fact, it got to the point where George and Don did not want to be together in the studio at the same time, so one would work in the afternoon and the other at night. Bass player Jeff Pilson did his best to mediate and keep the peace. (Over a decade later, I would hire him to do a similar job, playing bass and doing what he could to keep the peace between drummer Jason Bonham and guitarist extraordinaire Zakk Wylde on the *Rock Star* movie project.)

To make matters worse, I was unaware that recording engineer Geoff Workman, who had engineered *Shout At The Devil*, was telling George on the side that I had no idea what I was doing—that I had no knowledge of the guitar, and that he, Geoff, would do everything he possibly could by himself to save the album. (He had apparently done this same thing with Nikki Sixx, and he would do it again with Dee Snider when I hired him to engineer the Twisted Sister album. I canned him after that.)

In short, Geoff was a fine recording engineer, but he was also devious, deceptive, and destructive. He had secretly recorded hours of my conversations in the control room and edited them so that it sounded as though I was saying rude and nasty things about the band.

Because he was an excellent engineer, it must have sounded natural, and George swallowed both conversations: Geoff's real one and 'my' fake, reconstructed one.

The project had been going fairly well, under the circumstances. George had recorded his guitar parts to the song 'Tooth & Nail,' and I was knocked out by the lead break. I told him as much, and when he attempted a lead break for the next tune we did, I expressed my admiration for his speed and dexterity but said that I'd like it if his notes 'took me from point A to point B,' rather than having him just remain in one melodic place and 'shred' (although we didn't use that term at the time). I told him how the 'Tooth & Nail' solo had a great shape, and how the melody transported the listener from beginning to end.

George immediately took off his headphones, threw them to the floor, put down his guitar, and said, in so many words, that he 'wasn't gonna take it anymore.' He was furious. I invited him to come into the control room and take a swing at me if that would make him feel better. He declined, and I walked. Between his problem with Don, his problem with the material (he favored rockers while Don favored ballads), and his problem with me, I thought it best to quit—so I did. It was a shame, though, because a guitarist as good as George is a producer's dream.

The following morning I called the band's manager, Cliff Burnstein, and negotiated my way out. Cliff recruited veteran engineer Michael Wagener and producer Roy Thomas Baker to finish up the project; I went to Nantucket with my family for a couple of months, and Michael and Roy did a nice job completing the album, which went platinum.

To this day, George has nothing but negative things to say about me, but I still think he's one of the top ten rock guitar players in the world, and I still count that 'Tooth & Nail' guitar solo as one of the best I've ever heard.

CHAPTER TWENTY-ONE

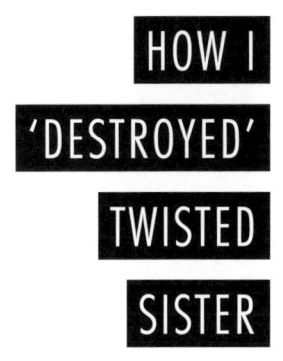

HOW I 'DESTROYED' TWISTED SISTER

In the fall of 1983, I received a call at home from Doug Morris, president of Atlantic Records. He said he had an American act on the label that had built a decent following in Europe, but they couldn't seem to get anything going stateside. 'I really believe you're the only producer who can make a hit with these guys,' he told me.

When a label president says something like this, you tend to respond positively. Doug asked me to see the band, and of course I agreed. Since Doug was directly involved, I knew that if I made a good record there would be a full-court press by the label, and Doug would take credit for a smart move.

I flew to Pennsylvania to see the band in a small club. They performed in front of a crude stage set depicting a back-alley urban scene, complete with a section of chain-link fence. It was unusual to see a stage set in a small rock club. Like KISS, this was a band that valued the importance of theater in live music. I admired their spirit and their attitude, and I found their songs refreshingly straightforward and basic, with few chord changes and lots of catchy, sing-along choruses. These were songs that would be relatively easy to arrange, and easy to make more interesting through the addition of harmony vocals, gang vocals, keyboards, percussion, and so on. It was basic rock'n'roll, but I was sure the material could benefit from a few good musical ideas.

We hung out a bit after the show, and the guys seemed to be enthusiastic about my involvement. I could see they were dedicated, committed to achieving success, and in it for the long haul. They were a homegrown Long Island band with a lot of pride, attitude, and a good local following, but not that many music buyers outside of the New York area were familiar with them.

Taking into consideration my schedule, the potential of the band, their unique presentation, and Doug Morris's personal involvement, I was happy to do the record. I liked the band members, too, and got along well with them.

At their request, we rehearsed on Long Island and recorded the basic tracks for what would become their third album, *Stay Hungry*, at the Record Plant in Manhattan. We set up the instruments and got good sounds on the drum kit and the bass guitar, and then we approached the rhythm guitar, played by the band's founder, Jay Jay French.

To dial in the best sound for an instrument, it would usually take about an hour to find the right microphones, the right positioning for them, and the right settings on the recording console. On that first day, however, we couldn't manage to get a guitar sound that Jay Jay or I liked, even though we worked on it for the entire afternoon and evening.

The struggle continued the next day; we rented a number of different guitars and guitar amps, but I went to bed that night still not having managed to get what I considered a good rhythm guitar sound. When I awoke in my hotel room on the third morning, I was pretty depressed, and wasn't at all happy about going to the studio—in fact, I didn't even want to get out of bed. Through it all, though, Jay Jay was patient and cooperative. He told me he didn't know that much about what equipment might provide a sound that would make us happy.

Jay Jay and bassist Mark 'The Animal' Mendoza were the voices of reason in the band, and Jay Jay was the band's de facto business manager. I enjoyed my working relationship with these two, and with guitarist Eddie Ojeda and drummer A.J. Pero. They took direction well, worked hard, and had a strong allegiance to the band. Under Jay Jay's positive leadership, they forged a solid and cohesive unit that sometimes seemed almost patriotic in their love for and pride in Twisted Sister. Jay Jay was a reasonable guy who said what he meant and meant what he said.

I was also impressed by the band's dedication to exercise, bodybuilding, and wellness. When it came to drugs, tobacco, and alcohol, frontman Dee Snider had a similar attitude to Ted Nugent, albeit more dictatorial. While I know that a couple of the boys secretly indulged (I know this because I indulged with them), they were primarily into weight lifting and exercise—hence the phrase 'Stay Hungry,' which, as they explained to me, was the bodybuilders' credo: *Never satisfy your craving for food. If you're always a little hungry, you'll never overeat, and you'll stay fit.* 'Lean and mean,' however, was not their thing. 'Big and bruising' was more like it.

Maybe this concentration on pumping iron and pumping up was compensation for the band's image, which involved a measure of androgyny; maybe they wanted people to know that the mascara and rouge were strictly for show and not a sign of gender ambiguity. At any rate, they gave Molly Hatchet a run for their money in the 'toughest band' category. Mark was particularly ominous in his appearance—this was clearly a guy you wouldn't want to piss off. In reality, though, he was Mark Glickman, a nice Jewish boy from Long Island.

When the album was over, the band resumed touring. While vacationing on the east coast that summer, I took my wife and young daughter up to an outdoor gig of theirs in nearby New Hampshire. After the show, we waited outside the band's tour bus so we could say hello. It was a very hot and humid New England summer day, but we waited patiently in the blazing sun for at least a half-hour. The band members were on the tour bus, and they knew we were waiting outside in the ninety-degree heat, but no one ever came out—not even to tell us we weren't welcome. I never understood why—and of course Dee Snider and I have not spoken since then.

* * *

Poor Dee—so many people to blame, and so little time. After smiling his way through all the recording sessions with nary a complaint—and, more importantly, after approving all of the final mixes—he went on to repeatedly proclaim his disdain for me.

Here's an excerpt from an interview Snider did with *Classic Rock* magazine in 2004: 'Snider is adamant that not only was Tom Werman the wrong guy, but that the album would have exploded no matter who had been behind the console. "We'd have been as huge as we became, no matter what," he believes. "Using some pop producer was not the key to having a hit record. Tom told me that he worked with us for the money. At least he was honest. The sickening part is that the guy still gets royalties from us."'

In actual fact, I worked with Twisted Sister because Doug Morris asked me to, because I thought they were capable of making a hit record, and because I could help them make it. Only a fool would tell a band that he was only in it for the money. But it's amusing that he weaves a tale and then says that I was 'honest' in saying it. We're deep in Trumpland here.

Here's what Snider told Blabbermouth.com in 2020: 'Tom Werman, who produced *Stay Hungry*, he produced [Mötley] Crüe, he produced [Ted] Nugent, he produced Cheap Trick, Molly Hatchet, Poison ... he produced so many bands. He's got, like, fifteen platinum albums to his credit. He walked into the studio, and he says, *I don't touch the board. I don't write. I don't create. I'll just tell you if I like it or not.* [And he was taking] eight points—eight freakin' points.'

By that, he means eight percentage points as a royalty on sales of the record; in plain fact, no producer in the world ever received eight points on any record. But the guy was apparently committed to making me look bad.

After reading various things about Snider's contempt for me, I emailed him twice to request a guest spot on his local radio show, so that we could have a candid on-air conversation. He never replied; I wasn't surprised.

Meanwhile, a friend told me about some of the claims Snider makes in his book; among other things, he writes that my being hired to produce their record was the beginning of a 'butterfly effect' that eventually destroyed the band!

A butterfly effect? The Wikipedia definition is 'the sensitive dependence on initial conditions in which a small change in one state of a deterministic nonlinear system can result in large differences in a later state.' Does Dee have a PhD in comparative philosophy?

I'm aware that inner politics and discord can break up a band, but a producer who worked with members of a band for a mere two months out of their career must have had an enormous impact if the band goes into the project as a cohesive group, but then, as a result of that producer's involvement, breaks up a few months later.

I spent six weeks with Twisted Sister, and Snider apparently wasn't able to save the band from my destructive influence, even though he had been the band's leader for over ten years.

Trash-talking isn't unusual for people with a poor self-image. Given his penchant for historical revision and his apparent ability to recall twenty-five-year-old conversations word-for-word, I'm honored to occupy a premier position on his shit list.

Stay Hungry was easily the most challenging project of the more than fifty albums I produced, but it was a big hit, and I was fairly curious about Snider's resentment after the album had sold millions of records. He ridiculed me in the press for suggesting that they cover a tune by Saxon, a British metal band, proclaiming that he was amazed at my suggestion that his band could cover someone else's song—especially a song by one of the bands they had toured with. So what did they release as the first single from their next album? A cover version of 'Leader Of The Pack,' a lightweight pop song from the 60s.

Meanwhile, despite declaring that I had 'destroyed' the album, Snider would then praise the record to the skies in an interview with examiner.com in 2009:

> It's amazing to see the significance of the record, you know the original, and how many times I hear people saying, 'This was my primer to heavy metal'... 'We're Not Gonna Take It' was added at 145 radio stations the first week it came out, and that was two weeks before the video even hit. And just so you know, that's a lot of radio stations to play a heavy metal band in 1984.... One thing a lot of people have said was, '*Stay Hungry* was Twisted Sister's go-commercial, selling out.' And I always laugh because it was anything but.

Sorry I destroyed your record, Dee. It's interesting to note that Twisted Sister chose Dieter Dierks, well known for his work with the metal band Scorpions, to produce their next album, *Come Out And Play*. While *Stay Hungry* has sold over five million copies, their follow-up has sold far fewer. And that's with guest appearances by Billy Joel, Alice Cooper, and Clarence Clemons.

It's a rare occurrence for the follow-up to a multi-million-selling album to be a poor seller. The fact that I was involved in their only big hit seems to follow Dee around like a big dark cloud.

CHAPTER TWENTY-ONE

Andrew Hickey, the man behind the wonderful podcast *The History Of Rock Music In 500 Songs*, said about rock stars:

> The scene was not one that would tend to produce particularly nice people, simply because it involved taking charismatic but often rather damaged young men still in or barely out of adolescence, telling them they're geniuses, giving them large amounts of amphetamines, and then fulfilling their every narcissistic desire. It's honestly amazing that any of them were even remotely tolerable human beings at all.

CHAPTER TWENTY-TWO

FAMILY MAN

My professional life was hardly that of a typical working dad. Suky and I had started a family just a year after I joined CBS. Our daughters, Julia and Nina, were born while we were living a few miles over the George Washington Bridge in the small New Jersey suburb of Leonia, the first town on the Jersey side of the bridge; since we could only afford one car, I commuted year-round to work in Midtown Manhattan on a Honda 350cc motorcycle, which I parked for a dollar a day in an underground garage a block from Epic Records.

We rented a small carriage house behind a big house on a quiet, tree-lined street. My city life and my home life were completely separate. I had a city persona and a Jersey persona. I'd come in with the commuter crowd down the West Side Highway and sometimes return home in the very late evening after Suky and the kids had gone to sleep.

By contrast, when we moved to LA, our home was just twenty minutes from the studios, twenty minutes from the clubs I'd visit after work to see bands, and twenty minutes from most of the record-label headquarters. Suky would bring the kids down to the studio for dinner; they'd return to the house and I'd return to the studio, where my life was in stark contrast to my peaceful nest on Laurel Hills Road.

The Werman girls were comfortable with hard rock, heavy metal, and the people involved in it. They were used to having leather-clad rockers at the house, and they loved having great seats and backstage passes at concerts. In our home, someone was always playing music. Our son Daniel, currently a senior VP of A&R at Warner Records, has been keenly focused on music all his life, both as a fan and as a collector.

Early on, though, Dan did have a couple of issues. He found it difficult to understand the concept of men with very long hair. Every time Eddy Grant's 'Electric Avenue' would come on MTV, Dan would dash out of the room, and when Dee Snider appeared once at our front door, Dan ran up the stairs and waited in his bedroom until Dee left. As Snider's producer, I, unfortunately, wasn't permitted to do this.

Over time, the Werman kids got used to the rock'n'roll life. Dan learned how to play the drums on a mongrel drum kit consisting largely of Tommy Lee's castoffs. Ted Nugent stood astride our standard poodle Max and 'rode' him around the house, yelling 'yee-haw.' And when Cheap Trick was in town, Rick Nielsen would come over occasionally, and on one Halloween evening our kids went out trick-or-treating together in Studio City. (Later in life, one of those two little kids would replace Bun E. Carlos and play drums for Cheap Trick.) My kids enjoyed a certain notoriety at school because of their dad. High school boys loved Mötley Crüe, and high school girls adored Bret Michaels. At North Hollywood High, you just didn't mess with Julia Werman—her dad was 'tight with the Crüe.'

In 1985, we bought a couple of acres near the beach on Nantucket and built a vacation home. We'd move the whole family and our two dogs to the island every summer for six weeks. This getaway was a treasured period of renewal, a return to a relatively healthy lifestyle, and uninterrupted time with the family. At that point I was able to arrange my work schedule on my own terms; I did three projects a year, starting in September and ending in June. If a band absolutely had to work in July and August, I'd pass on the project.

* * *

One summer, while going through Logan Airport in Boston on our way to Nantucket, seven-year-old Dan spotted a couple of tall men in full-length black leather coats, wearing sunglasses, their long hair pulled back. He pointed at them and, echoing a frequent joke of mine, said, 'Dad, I bet those guys worship the devil.' Recognizing my old KISS acquaintants, Gene Simmons and Paul Stanley, I took Dan's hand and said, 'Let's find out.' He was reluctant. I brought him over to them and said, 'Hey, my son thinks you guys worship the devil.' As he stared in wonder at the two men towering over us in their platform boots, a very uncomfortable Dan was relieved to learn that they were acquaintances.

The Crüe spent a lot of time on the road; one day in a stroke of genius, I told Vince I'd be happy to keep his Harley Davidson Softail Custom while he was away; I assured him that I'd keep this $10,000 bike sheltered, clean and shiny, and have it tuned up for his homecoming at a nearby Harley dealer. Better to run it frequently than to leave it stationary in some garage for 3 or 4 months, right? Vince agreed, and I'd go out riding on weekends.

I was driving a Porsche Carrera at that time, and if I did anything on the road that could be considered aggressive by other drivers, they wouldn't hesitate to flip me off and express their disdain; but when I was cruising on Vince's Harley, it was a different story. People gave me thumbs up or a raised fist, and if I pulled over to ask directions, they'd recoil as if I might bludgeon them to death. I got a lot of respect, simply because of what I was sitting on. It was 'right on' all the way, and this was proof positive that in LA there was truth to the phrase, 'You are what you drive.'

On occasional mornings, after the kids finished breakfast, Suky would give Julia a bowl of hot water and a face cloth to bring to me in bed before she left for school. I'd put the hot cloth across my forehead to ease the throbbing—a result of the previous night's merriment. Not knowing what a hangover was at her young age, Julia assumed this was something all daughters routinely did for their fathers.

Later on, I had a two-person sauna installed in our bedroom closet so I could sweat out the previous night's toxins before I left for the studio. I'd call ahead and ask the runner to get me a double cheeseburger and well-done fries for a nutritious noon breakfast. Grease and animal fat somehow helped to soothe a hangover. Then there would be an afternoon of smoking and working in a windowless room, followed by five o'clock cocktails, dinner with several glasses of wine, and back into the studio for a late evening fueled by Jack Daniels and cocaine.

To counteract this suicidal regimen, I'd take a week from time to time to clean up, and I regularly ran through the hills on the fire trail near our house. It was a serious run, powered by the playlist I recorded on my Sony Walkman. I figured that this righteous physical activity provided me with permission to misbehave during the following weeks, until it was time for the next cleanse.

As I left for work around noon and returned sometime after midnight, I never encountered rush-hour traffic. The studio would be a workplace in the afternoon and something of a party room at night. We usually got most of our best work done between 8pm and midnight. If I encountered a police cruiser on the drive home, I'd pull up right beside and wave hello; this effectively indicated to them that I wasn't under the influence.

I was late to the party in terms of sobering up and getting my act together, thanks in great part to my sheltered upbringing and the joy I derived from finally escaping its bonds. And so it went for about fifteen years until my poor body just couldn't deal with the constant assault of unfriendly input. By age forty-five, it would typically take a full three days for me to purge the effects of a night of partying. Most of my friends and colleagues had cleaned up years earlier. As for me, better late than never.

CHAPTER TWENTY-THREE

ALMOST McCARTNEY, GUNS N' ROSES

Sitting in my Laurel Canyon kitchen one sunny weekday afternoon between projects, the phone rang, and a gentleman's voice on the other end asked, 'Hello, is this Tom Werman?'

I answered yes, and he introduced himself, telling me his name and saying that he was calling from Paul McCartney's office in London. I smiled, wondering who this might be. Whoever it was, he was good; he spoke with a genuine British accent, and his voice had the ambient, echoey sound of a transatlantic call.

'Paul would like to know if you might be available to work on a project starting in April.' It had to be a joke, of course, but there was something about the man's tone that kept me from asking, 'Who is this, anyway?'

I chuckled, signifying to him that I was either incredulous or amused.

'Well, I think I could manage to make myself available for Paul,' I replied with a laugh.

The man simply thanked me and prepared to hang up.

Suddenly realizing there was a very slim chance that the call might be genuine, I said, 'Can I ask why you're calling *me*?'

'Well,' he replied, 'Paul likes to keep all of his options open.' Then he thanked me, I thanked him, and that was it. The whole exchange lasted less than a minute.

I immediately called Sandy Roberton, who was managing me at the time, and told him the man's name and the nature of our conversation. Sandy was British and well-connected. He told me he'd make a few calls, then phoned me back a few minutes later to assure me that yes, the call was genuine.

I told Suky what had just happened, and the two of us sat there and tried to digest this experience. I never heard from the man again, but I was flabbergasted that Paul McCartney even knew—and had spoken—my name. I eventually came to assume that his daughter Stella, a teenager at the time, must have had one of my records—maybe a Cheap Trick album—and suggested that her father check it out. Apparently, John Lennon knew of Cheap Trick, too. In an interview, Bun E. Carlos reported that when he and Rick Nielsen arrived at the Record Plant in New York after Jack Douglas invited them to work with John on *Double Fantasy*, John said 'Oh, you're the guys from Cheap Trick. They told me your names, but they didn't tell me what band you were from.'

Even as I sat there with time on my hands and not a whole lot of interest from the industry, the fact that one of The Beatles knew who Cheap Trick was, and who I was, lifted my spirits for months afterward.

* * *

My former associate Tom Zutaut left Elektra Records shortly after I did; I became an independent producer, and he joined the Geffen Records A&R staff. One day in 1986, he phoned to ask if I would check out a new band he had acquired for the label. The band was called Guns N' Roses.

Tom had signed them after seeing them play a showcase performance at the Roxy. They were creating quite a buzz back then, and many big-label A&R people were present. Tom knew very well how the A&R game was played. As soon as the band finished the first song, the story goes, he was sure this could be a grand slam, and he anticipated a big backstage scene after the show, with all the label reps trying to get the inside track. He also knew that he was well known in the industry and that others would be watching for his reaction to the band. So, after a few songs, he rose from his seat, slipped backstage and left instructions for the band to call his office in the morning, and then strolled out of the club, poker-faced. By leaving, he gave the impression that he wasn't interested—and this simple maneuver put enough doubt in the minds of his competition to clear the way for Tom to co-sign the band to Geffen Records the following morning.

After Tom called, I grabbed my recording engineer, Duane Baron, and we went over to a tiny rehearsal room just off the Sunset Strip. The room was separated from the sidewalk by a single door, and since no one could hear us knocking over the muffled roar from inside, we walked in. A couple of the guys looked over at us, but the band didn't stop playing. The volume was truly deafening. There were four musicians, but no vocalist. It was so incredibly loud in there that the actual key of the songs seemed to float. It was the Doppler effect—you couldn't pin it down. When they stopped playing, I introduced myself and Duane and asked where their singer was.

'He doesn't rehearse with us because we can't hear him,' bass player Duff McKagan replied. 'He can't hear himself, either.'

Some months before I attended this rehearsal, McKagan had visited one of our Mötley Crüe sessions at Conway Recorders, and he seemed nice enough. One of the Mötley guys had invited him down, and I introduced myself and offered him a seat. I was involved with the session, so we didn't have any further conversation. He sat quietly and observed the proceedings from the side of the control room. He stayed for ten or fifteen minutes and then left.

Guns N' Roses went through several more songs. The enormous volume in the tiny room forced me to put my hands over my ears to reduce the din of the highest frequencies—something I frequently did so I could hear the music more clearly. After a few more songs with no vocals, I thanked the band and explained to them that I really should come back another time to hear them with the singer, since it was impossible to evaluate songs without the vocals. This could have been taken as a sarcastic comment, but I meant what I said. Zutaut was probably not aware that there would be no singer at the rehearsal. But as far as evaluating the band was concerned, this had not been very productive.

Before I had the chance to pay the band a second visit, they chose to have Mike Clink produce their first album. Mike was a hardworking, friendly young guy I knew from the Record Plant, where he had graduated from assistant to recording engineer. He made a wonderful record with the band. I couldn't have done better.

After the album was released, I read a magazine interview with the band in which McKagan reported that when I came to see them in rehearsal I put my hands over my ears, said, 'Oh, fuck,' and walked out of the room without saying a word.

Aside from the fact that this was utter fiction (why did musicians enjoy making up demeaning stories about their producers?) and obviously meant to embarrass me and make me look like a jerk, he made no mention of the painful volume, the absence of a singer, or our brief conversation at the time. He made it seem as if I just hated the music and rudely walked out. It was a lie, plain and simple. I still haven't a clue as to how I pissed him off.

I ran into him at another band's record release party a few weeks later and asked him why he had lied about me to the magazine's writer. Visibly drunk, he loudly demanded to know if I was calling him a liar—which I was—and then threatened to hit me. This was amusing, as he was about half a foot taller and twenty-five years younger than I was.

Months later, I was doing a session at A&M Studios, and Mike Clink happened to be working there that day. I walked into his control room to see if I could borrow a piece of equipment. I was unaware that all of Guns N' Roses was in there, too. Immediately, McKagan started trash-talking and insulting me. Feeling uncomfortable, Mike motioned for me to step out into the hall so we could speak in peace.

I never did find out why the kid hated me. A few years later, I was invited to Slash's house in Beverly Hills to discuss the possibility of my producing a solo album for him. In stark contrast to McKagan, Slash was a total gentleman—articulate, polite, confident, and soft-spoken. He complimented me on my body of work, asked if I was working on anything at the time, offered me food and drink, and showed me his remarkable collection of snakes. He eventually chose to work with another producer.

That was the extent of my experience with Guns N' Roses. I never found out the reason behind McKagan's stream of verbal abuse, and because they were always so late to go onstage, I never once saw the band perform.

CHAPTER TWENTY-FOUR

POISON: NOTHIN' BUT A GOOD TIME

'Gorilla': *a popular record industry term used by promotion men to describe a giant hit record.*

Mötley Crüe's *Girls, Girls, Girls* was released in the spring of 1987 and went to #2 on the *Billboard* 200. By that time, I'd been producing gold or platinum albums for fifteen years. Labels considered me a good investment, and it was largely for this reason that I was approached by Capitol Records to meet with Poison, whose first album had been a big surprise hit.

I was contacted by Capitol A&R man Tom Whalley, who later served as head of A&R and ultimately president at Interscope Records, and then went on to the presidency of Warner Bros Records. Poison had been just another Hollywood glam band until their debut album, heavily supported by MTV exposure, generated three chart singles. They were signed to the Enigma label, which was distributed by Capitol, and their hit album was Enigma's biggest-selling album to date.

That first album was produced by Ric Browde, who fifteen years earlier had been an assistant to Lew Futterman, Ted Nugent's original manager/producer, back when Lew and I were working together on Ted's albums. In those days, Ric would get coffee and do errands for Lew, but he'd come a long way since then, and he certainly did a pretty good job making Poison's first album. The band, however, told Tom Whalley they wanted Paul Stanley to produce their follow-up record. Since Paul was unavailable, Whalley turned to me.

Poison's manager, Tom Mohler, arranged a lunch meeting at the

Sunset Strip restaurant Le Dome so that the band and I could become acquainted. I was seated next to guitar player C.C. Deville, a funny and warm guy, and the band's resident clown. At one point he turned to me and said, 'So, Mr. Werman'—he always called me Mr. Werman—'I hear you do drugs.' Having heard some fascinating tales about Mr. Deville's own drug use, I found this a little amusing.

'I like to party as much as the next guy,' I replied, 'but I take my work seriously, and my work always comes first.' I believed what I said, and I remember thinking that maybe he was hoping I'd become his drug buddy in the studio. My reply seemed to satisfy him, and the band agreed to have me produce their record.

A couple of months later, in the middle of a pre-recording rehearsal at a big San Fernando Valley sound stage one afternoon, the band's singer, Bret Michaels, told me he'd like to play me a song he'd just written. I handed him my acoustic Guild D55—the one my first Epic boss, Larry Cohn, had bought me back in 1970—and Bret sat down and quietly strummed 'Every Rose Has Its Thorn.' As I mentioned earlier, I don't always recognize a hit on the first listen, but this one was different; this one sounded like an undeniable hit right away, and I told Bret as much. It also felt like a country song, but I didn't mention that. Years later, Miley Cyrus covered it. I did tell him I'd love to have it on the album, and that I'd like him to play the rhythm guitar part—to strum it on my Guild guitar exactly the way we had all just heard it in rehearsal.

Usually, C.C. played all the guitar parts—rhythm and lead—but Bret seemed to have a natural feel for this song, and I wanted to capture that feel on tape. Aside from being a good singer and guitar player, Bret also played a pretty decent harmonica.

I went home to dinner that night feeling reassured that before we even walked into the studio we were pretty sure we had at least one strong single on the album. Considering 'Every Rose' and a few of the other tunes we were rehearsing, I began to think we may be looking at a 'gorilla' here. 'Every Rose Has Its Thorn' would turn out to be the only #1 chart song in my career.

After pre-production and rehearsals with the band, I chose to record the album on digital tape rather than on analog magnetic tape. While there had been much discussion about the merits of each, I was sure there would be a large number of re-records and corrections (punch-ins), partly due to what I heard at our rehearsals, and partly due to what I had been told about the band's propensity to have 'nothin' but a good time.' Going over the same spot again and again on analogue tape, which recorded sound magnetically, could damage the tape. If the tape ran across the 'record' or 'erase' or 'playback' head too many times, the backing could begin to flake off. Digital tape was more durable; one could go in and out of the 'record' mode seamlessly and endlessly.

For the Poison session, I'd sit in the chair at the recording console, placing my fingers on the remote control, just as a touch typist places fingers on a keyboard, and spend hours recording a thirty-second guitar solo until it was perfect.

C.C. displayed flashes of virtuosity on the guitar, but his recreational habits during the making of that album diminished his focus and performance considerably. And Bret had so many women visiting him in the studio that I suggested he set up one of those machines you find at the delicatessen outside the control room, so I could open the door and shout, 'Number twelve! Number twelve, next!'

One night, Duane Baron and I were discussing something at the console, and Bret was on the couch behind us working on some lyrics. Out of the corner of my eye, I saw one of his female admirers, who was hanging on his shoulder, turn to whisper in his ear; and then we heard Bret quietly reply, 'Listen, hon, I'm a little busy now. Could you just take care of my producer?' She seemed reluctant to make that particular move, which saved me the discomfort of having to turn down whatever she might have offered—but I appreciated Bret's generosity.

Bass player Bobby Dall was the de facto leader of the band and the one who managed the business side of things. While he appeared to be the serious one in the group, he did enjoy partying, and I witnessed at least one performance where he had to have assistance from the crew in order to exit the stage. Rikki Rocket always appeared to be a good timer, but he had a seriousness of purpose that belied his party posture. Rikki was a down-to-earth guy who was always candid. He once told me that he didn't consider himself to be the best drummer in the world, but he insisted on doing all the drumming on the record himself, and he gave it everything he had.

While we were rehearsing a song one afternoon, I asked Rikki to change a particular drum fill that he was used to playing at a specific spot in the song. He agreed to try what I suggested, but he didn't feel comfortable with it. Instead of refusing to play it or changing it so that it was easier for him to play, he sat and worked at it repeatedly for minutes on end until he mastered it. It wasn't something he would have come up with, but he was agreeable to trying it, and he simply hammered it out the hard way until he could play it the way I wanted to hear it. A producer appreciates a work ethic like that.

Poison may not have been the very best musicians I'd worked with, but they were dedicated to their work, and without any extraordinary effort on my part or theirs, we managed to record an album—*Open Up And Say...Ahh!*—which had four Top 10 singles. Not one of the other albums I produced yielded this many hits.

All in all, the members of Poison were diligent, good-natured, and a pleasure to work with. If only they had all been like that.

SIDE E
BURNING OUT

CHAPTER TWENTY-FIVE

THE DECLINE

The four phases of the record business:

1. 'Who's Tom Werman?'
2. 'Get me Tom Werman.'
3. 'Get me a young Tom Werman.'
4. 'Who's Tom Werman?'

One day during the Poison sessions, I was on my way out of the house when I heard the Beastie Boys' '(You Gotta) Fight For Your Right (To Party)' coming from my daughter Julia's room. Curious, I turned around, and from the door to her room I asked, 'Jules, how can you listen to that? It sounds like it was recorded in fifteen minutes.'

'But Dad,' she replied, 'that's just it.'

Uh oh.

Suddenly everything I knew was wrong. From that day on, I could see the writing on the wall. I had always strived for perfection in the studio; as far as I was concerned, to achieve power in music, you needed a consistent tempo, properly tuned instruments, tight musicianship, and pitch-perfect vocals. Without this control, music lost its power in the disorder and chaos—it was just messy. But the people making the new wave of music—that which quickly replaced what we knew as metal, hard rock, power pop, or 'corporate' rock—considered those aforementioned musical properties unnecessary and, eventually, undesirable.

In the movie *20th Century Women*, a single mom enters her teenage son's room while he and his girlfriend are sitting on the floor enjoying some loud, angry punk rock. In an effort to understand their alien teenage lifestyle, the mom says of the music, 'They're not very good, and they know that, right?'

'Yeah,' the girlfriend replies. 'It's like they've got all this feeling and they don't have any skill, and they don't want skill, because it's really interesting what happens when your passion is bigger than the tools you have to deal with it. It creates this energy that's raw. Isn't it great?'

Ultimately, Nirvana's brilliant *Nevermind* album initiated the decline of my career. I accepted that commercial rock had experienced a major shift in style, and at that point, I stopped searching for new music. I listened almost exclusively to music from the 60s, 70s, and 80s—as I still do—because it never got old for me; it creates memories of my youth, and it moves me emotionally. Also, there was music of that era that I had not yet heard. I listened to the music I was making in the studio but had time for very little else. If you've been listening to music for ten hours straight, when you get home at midnight you don't want to put on more music in order to relax.

In the years following the Poison project, I had enough work to keep me busy, but the artists weren't as commercially potent as the ones I had produced in the 80s. The demand for the style of music that I was heavily associated with was weakening, and I certainly wasn't regarded as cutting-edge, groundbreaking, or trendsetting.

During the 90s, I produced albums for bands like Love Hate, Stryper, Lita Ford, LA Guns, Glass Tiger, Babylon A.D., and three new bands on Geffen Records—Hash, Junkyard, and Pariah. The LA Guns album went gold, and the Glass Tiger album went gold in Canada, but none of the others sold very well, and the three Geffen albums made little or no impact at all. I enjoyed working with all these people, but the demand for 80s-style music just wasn't there.

I was pretty discouraged by this, because the one time I had met

David Geffen, he'd said, 'I'm a big fan. Why don't you make more records for us?'

'Well,' I replied, 'I guess you'd have to ask your A&R people.'

It would be nice to have delivered a hit record for Mr. Geffen.

* * *

I wasn't familiar with Stryper when I received their phone call, but I did know that they were the only Christian band that had sold a lot of records. Why were they calling me? I considered asking them if they knew I was neither Christian nor particularly Godfearing, but before I could do that, they explained that they wanted to make a secular album that had no religious messages or overtones. It seemed that I might qualify as an equal opportunity producer, having worked with a band that was associated with the devil himself, and then with a band that was pretty tight with the son of God.

The members of Stryper were the brothers Michael and Robert Sweet—guitar/vocalist and drummer, respectively—along with guitarist Oz Fox and bassist Tim Gaines. Michael and Robert's mother managed the band at the time, and I was invited to their house down in politically conservative Orange County, south of Los Angeles. Democrats spoke of the region as being "Behind the Orange Curtain"—in the 1990s, it was still Nixon country. We sat in the living room, and Mrs. Sweet brought out a platter of bagels, lox, and cream cheese. They clearly wanted me to feel at home.

I was pleased with the album we made, titled *Against The Law*; it was fairly heavy and metallic, with what I thought were a lot of Van Halen influences, and that could have been one of the reasons it wasn't a hit. This was a sound that, at the time, wasn't as popular or as much in demand as it had been ten years earlier.

Coincidentally, Michael has since collaborated with George Lynch,

Tracii Guns, and the band Boston—all part of my past. The Stryper guys were among the nicest people I ever worked with.

By the time I got to the LA Guns album *Cocked & Loaded* in 1989, I was happy to continue involving my recording engineer Duane Baron and his good friend John Purdell as co-producers. I admitted to myself that I wasn't sufficiently excited about several of the songs we were recording, and on some earlier projects (notably Poison's *Open Up And Say . . . Ahh!* and KIX's *Blow My Fuse* and *Hot Wire*) Duane, John, and I had made a very effective three-man team. John was a big help with vocal production, arranging, and keyboards. I was confident that he and Duane could handle production on the songs that I wasn't into. Fortunately, as the 'producer of record,' I was able to select my favorite songs and leave the remaining ones for them.

They handled 'The Ballad Of Jayne,' which did get to #33 on the *Billboard* Hot 100. My favorite from that album was 'Rip And Tear,' which I produced, and which featured some dazzling guitar shredding by Tracii Guns for the last minute of the song.

Lita Ford had been a member of The Runaways, a pioneering all-girl group who recorded five albums and then broke up just a few months before my family's move to LA. Lita joined the band as their lead guitarist, and Joan Jett moved to rhythm guitar. Later, as a solo artist, Lita made several successful records under the management of Ozzy's wife, Sharon Osbourne. But in 1991, when I recorded her, the hard-rock guitar sound had been replaced by 'alternative' music, ushered in by Nirvana's *Nevermind* album.

Drummer and co-songwriter Myron Grombacher had worked with Lita previously and was a big help in the studio, both on song arranging and drumming. He also had one of the most positive personalities of anyone I ever encountered in any recording studio.

Lita had some difficulties with pitch when she got in front of the microphone to do her vocals. She didn't like the earphones that singers usually use, so we tried putting two small speakers facing each other, with the microphone precisely at the midpoint between them; when we played the music track for her to sing to, the theory was that the opposing speakers would cancel the music out and make it inaudible to the microphone. That didn't do the trick either. Lita was a very good singer—she had earned a Grammy nomination in the 'Best Rock Vocal Performance By A Female Artist' category—so the pitch problem presented something of a mystery.

Finally, we recorded all the vocals—flats and sharps included—and decided to put them through a keyboard synthesizer with a pitch wheel, then record the manually pitch-corrected result on another track. I came in early for about a week; we'd listen to Lita's vocals line by line and note all the flat or sharp lyrics. Then we'd record the vocals on a new track while I nudged the pitch wheel up or down, depending on whether the word was flat or sharp. This was a tedious process, but it worked perfectly.

One song, 'Shot Of Poison,' was the most commercial tune on the album; it did crack the Hot 100 for a few weeks, but it was her last charting single release, and the album, *Dangerous Curves*, didn't make it into the Top 100 on the *Billboard* chart. It was a sobering experience for me, and I felt bad for Lita. I thought that I had done a good job on the record, but apparently, this music wasn't what people wanted to hear in 1991.

* * *

By the mid-90s, glam and metal music had become something of a joke, and I was getting pretty tired of the same old grind. I had more time between projects, and I awoke every morning with the same uncomfortable feeling that while all my friends were going to work, I had little or nothing to do that day. My self-esteem certainly wasn't at the level it had been at a decade earlier. I spent more time on the golf course, and I started thinking about doing something new—specifically, opening a sandwich shop on Ventura Boulevard in Studio City.

Before I did any work on the sandwich shop, however, I had an idea for a new and different music industry position. I would gather a group of the hippest and most influential music professionals in all the big urban music markets, have them seek out the best unsigned bands from their cities, and send me demos of these bands. From there, I'd put together a monthly cassette of the most promising unsigned acts in the country, and provide this cassette to labels on a subscription basis.

First, I'd need to convince record labels that this was a cost-saving and efficient way for them to find new talent, because they wouldn't need to send A&R men out to see the bands on location, paying for travel, room, and board. My network of tastemakers and talent scouts would serve as a giant nationwide A&R department. I'd reimburse these scouts for their expenses, and if any one of the acts they sent me was signed to a label, the scouts would get a bonus. If no demo was available, I might decide to go see the act in person. The price of a subscription to this service would be substantial. My talent scouts would be music critics of local newspapers, local deejays, musicians, club owners or booking agents, and so forth.

Unfortunately, there were two major flaws in this scheme—first, the labels would all hear the same acts at the same time, which could lead to bidding wars for the same acts; and second, the local talent scouts weren't salaried, so there was no guarantee that they would do any talent-scouting for me at all unless the signing bonus I offered was huge. Although I did travel to several cities and speak with several people who were interested in joining my network, the plan never got off the ground.

Since it was clear to me that my recording career had peaked, I thought I'd try to realize this other dream of mine, which was to open the best sandwich shop in LA; I'd call it Tommy's Lunch. I attended fancy food shows, found a baker at the San Francisco Culinary Institute to make artisan bread, and researched sources for the best meats, chips, pickles, coleslaw, potato salad, and the very best condiments. I began to look for a storefront on Ventura Boulevard, right in Studio City. Despite my MBA, I wasn't really qualified to do anything other than to make records or to make a really good sandwich. And now, I thought, it was time to leave the studio and come in from the cold, like a CIA operative who trades the international spy game for a less demanding desk job at Langley.

Then my friend John Baruck, manager of REO Speedwagon and later road manager for Journey and Christina Aguilera, called to tell me he'd recommended me as head of A&R at a new EMI startup label that would put together 'best of' albums, retrospectives, and boxed sets from the extensive Capitol / EMI artist catalogue, as well as producing new music to be marketed in novel ('alternative') ways. I met with marketing executive Bruce Kirkland at EMI-owned Capitol Records; Bruce was to run this new division, and he offered me a two-year contract to be head of the A&R department. This department would have access to most of the recordings by acts in the Capitol and Virgin catalogues (except for a few, including The Beatles).

In addition to these compilations, we found out that PGA golf champion Peter Jacobsen (winner of the US Open in 1995) had put together a novelty band called Jake Trout & The Flounders, consisting of himself, Payne Stewart (a two-time winner of the US Open), and PGA Tour player Mark Lye. Bruce wanted me to produce an album for this novelty group, which would be marketed through golf-club pro shops nationally. Jacobsen was a pop music fan, a decent guitarist and a pretty good singer, and he called on all his golf-loving rock star friends to license him to re-record their hit songs with new lyrics from a golfer's perspective, so 'I Love LA' became 'I Love To Play,' 'Smuggler's Blues' became 'Struggler's Blues,' and 'Love The One You're With' became 'Love The One You Whiff.'

During the recording, I had artists like Stephen Stills and Graham Nash singing in the studio, Glenn Frey playing guitar and singing a verse on 'Struggler's Blues,' Alice Cooper singing on 'I'm On 18,' and Darius Rucker of Hootie & the Blowfish singing on 'I Just Wanna Cry.' I expected little more than a quick visit from big artists like these, so I wasn't prepared for Glenn to come in and work on the guitar solo for 'Struggler's Blues' for two hours.

I had played a couple of rounds of golf with him at the Kelly–Baruck Invitational, and I found him to be as considerate and modest as any musician I'd ever met. When I got together with him in the studio to work on 'Struggler's Blues,' he was focused and productive, while still allowing me to be the producer. After a couple of decades of identifying and correcting guitar players' musical errors, I wondered just how picky I could be with someone of Glenn's stature. Should I mention that little bend that didn't quite make it to the note he was aiming for? Or maybe that the D-string was just a touch flat? Would it irritate him?

When Glenn finished his first take, I thought I'd show him how good I was by pointing out three slightly flawed guitar figures that I thought he should fix; when we listened back, he noted those exact three figures, and then went on to mention three more that I hadn't even noticed. 'Let's do those too,' he said with a smile, 'just in case Henley hears this.' It turned out Glenn was considerably beyond me in terms of thoroughness and detail, and you can hear this care reflected in the near perfection of Eagles recordings.

I was very satisfied with what my musicians and I had accomplished in duplicating the various hits for the Jake Trout & The Flounders record, and Peter did a nice job of singing the revised lyrics. After the album was finished, Payne Stewart expressed his thanks to me for helping him to sound 'better than he was' and invited Bruce Kirkland and me down to Orlando to play eighteen holes with him at his home club, Isleworth. At that time, the club's members included Tiger Woods and three other US Open champions.

Sadly, my time at Capitol was almost up. EMI Records had a habit of sending their British personnel over to the States to solve what they perceived to be their American companies' problems, and in our case, their efforts destroyed the company. EMI closed down the label, and I was paid most of the balance of my contract after sixteen months... which of course afforded me even more time to play golf with my buddy Tom Kelly.

CHAPTER TWENTY-SIX

A RANT: MY DESPERATE ATTEMPT TO CONTINUE

In 1999, I had what I considered to be a great idea that would provide my last opportunity to do something creative in the music industry.

I had identified two areas that needed serious attention: the poor supervision of the recording process by inexperienced A&R people, and the obscene amount of money being wasted in making these records. I had seen it all: I'd spent millions of record company dollars and thousands of hours in the studio with musicians from the talented and serious to the marginally talented and drugged out.

Now I could be a consultant to record labels—a behind-the-scenes troubleshooter who could solve studio issues and teach young, inexperienced A&R men how to make better records for less money. This service would benefit the label's own A&R people, many of whom produced records themselves or oversaw the work of the independent producers they hired. I'd provide experienced ears, since I'd been on both sides—as a label employee who selected and supervised producers, and also as an independent producer who was hired by the label's A&R men. As a veteran of both roles, and the most experienced person on the label's creative staff, I could solve sticky problems in the studio—maybe a vocalist was having a hard time with pitch or phrasing, or a guitarist couldn't find the right amplifier for the sound he wanted, or the kick drum didn't have that certain thud they were looking for, or the mix wasn't quite right...

I planned to meet with all the record label presidents to convince them that the salary I had in mind would save them ten times that amount annually—and would provide the label's acts with a higher quality of music. I'd function as 'executive producer' for every album on which I consulted.

I was excited. I just needed to convince one label head. But I had no idea how difficult the selling process would be, even just in terms of scheduling a fifteen-minute appointment to pitch the idea.

After a year of failed attempts to meet with many label executives, I sat down at the computer in anger and frustration and pounded out what follows. The events are accurate and true; they may be difficult to believe, but it all happened just as described. You can skip it if you like, but here is a candid and painful glimpse into a very dark side of the record business.

* * *

Some successful CEOs and corporate executives are born with a priority order that places their own success far above personal relationships, above their own integrity, and in some cases above common decency. Some rock stars are like this, too. They'll spend months with you in close working conditions, go drinking with you, eat meals with you, laugh with you, high-five you, even confide in you and discuss their personal lives with you . . . yet somehow, despite this, they'll avoid forging any kind of meaningful bond with you. They befriend you at the time because you can help them to achieve their immediate musical goals, but later on, if you're not helping them to become more successful or more famous, you may as well never have existed.

So I'm looking for a new situation, and, as a job-seeker, I prepared a résumé, listing the key points of my career to date: how the acts I had signed to CBS Records collectively sold more than a hundred million albums; how I'd produced the records for several of the acts I signed, including each of those bands' biggest albums; and how, after working my way up from assistant to the director of A&R to senior VP and executive producer at CBS, I went to another label as senior VP of A&R, then became an independent producer, working on a total of twenty-three gold- and platinum-selling albums.

On paper, I thought I looked pretty good, right? Think again.

I sent my résumé to every major label in the country and to a couple in London, along with a description of my proposed job as 'senior A&R consultant.' I noted in my proposal that I could troubleshoot or consult on any aspect of a label's projects, function as a talent scout who was exclusive to the label, or produce all or part of any record for them. I'd be a jack of all creative trades.

Most of the label heads I approached didn't even bother to return my first phone call. Not one label in the industry was interested enough to take this concept beyond a single brief meeting—if I got that far. Not one senior executive or label head——many of whom I knew personally—would admit that his or her operation could benefit from what I was proposing.

Even worse than this was the indignity of the job search itself.

In the summer of 1994, I was at our place in Nantucket. I had just completed a Tora Tora LP for A&M, and for the first time in fifteen years, there were no new projects on the table. It seemed like a good time to reinvent myself. I was eager to rejoin an organization where I could interact with others who shared my love of music. I'd been out of the workplace and isolated in windowless control rooms for too long. I was ready to be an employee again, and I yearned to be back in an office. I was even willing to pick up and move back to New York. I discussed things with Suky, and she thought it would be okay if I tried to reenter the corporate world after fifteen years of independence.

In the spring of 1984 I had lunch with my friend Ron Stone, who had worked with David Geffen and then established Gold Mountain

Management with Danny Goldberg. 'Tom, take it from me,' he said. 'You really don't want a label job. Besides, record companies aren't interested in saving money, only in making it. Let me get you a production deal instead.'

I was willing to give this a shot, so Ron introduced me to a fellow named Brian, who worked in his office. Brian set up a meeting with Dave Massey, the VP of A&R at Epic in New York. Dave, who turned out to be a very nice guy, told me that Sony didn't favor production deals and that the terms weren't all that advantageous for the producer. I told him that a production deal hadn't been my original plan, and instead described the position I had conceived.

To my delight, Dave liked this idea very much. He said that I should meet with someone we'll call 'Margaret,' who served at the right hand of one of the label's chief executives, whom we'll call 'Jake'—and who seemed to be the one running Sony on a day-to-day basis.

Crossing 52nd Street after leaving Dave's office, I heard someone shout, 'Hey, Werman!' There was Jake himself, sitting in the back seat of a black Mercedes limo. I walked over to say hello and told him I had been in to see Dave Massey about this new position I was proposing.

'You're speaking to the wrong person,' Jake told me. 'You should be talking to Margaret about that. Call me later this afternoon.'

I had my doubts about this, but when I phoned Jake later, he picked right up. After a brief explanation of my proposal, he told me he would 'tell Margaret to take your call.' It was nice of him to do this, and of course he meant well, but I had no idea at the time that Dave's and Jake's calls to Margaret would prevent me from ever getting to first base with this self-absorbed woman.

After three phone calls to—but no return calls from—Margaret, one of her two assistants arranged for me to fly in from Nantucket for a meeting. I could tell Margaret was a very busy person as she had two assistants who repeatedly told me how very busy she was, and how sorry they were about how little time she had for me.

A couple of weeks later, I flew to New York and cabbed straight to the Sony offices at 550 Madison Avenue. I sat in the executive floor reception area for about thirty minutes with a number of Japanese businessmen in dark suits until Margaret finally emerged and informed me that an emergency had just arisen and that she was the only one who could fix it. (Trump was fond of saying that, too.) She said I could either have five minutes right then and there, or I could come back tomorrow morning. Not having planned to stay the night in the city, and feeling a bit like a nervous gameshow contestant, I decided to choose door number one and give it my best shot in the five minutes I had been allowed.

We sat down in a conference room next to her office. I described what I wanted to do and why it made good sense for me to come home to Sony and do it there; she listened and nodded, and then, after precisely five minutes, she walked me to the elevator. While I was disappointed at having been given only five minutes, I was encouraged by her apparent interest in hearing more. She said she actually liked the idea very much—especially the part about saving money—and that I should send her a written proposal.

I reported back to Brian, and the next day he told me that when he followed up with Margaret, she'd told him, too, that she liked the idea. So, maybe my friend Ron Stone was wrong—maybe record companies had grown cost-conscious in the more corporate 90s.

I returned to Nantucket and worked for three days on a very tight and well-thought-out job proposal, which I sent by fax and also by hard copy in the mail. I confirmed with one of Margaret's assistants that the proposal had arrived, and sat back to await her response. I wrote a thank you note to Jake for setting me up, and I started to think about how great it would be to work in New York again. I'd grown tired of LA's boring climate, and I missed the winter.

Weeks passed, then months. I phoned Margaret's office a number of times, and each time one of her assistants would tell me how busy she was and how little time she had. Poor woman.

In October, I informed Margaret's office that I would be in New York for a week and would be available for a follow-up meeting at her convenience, any time, any place.

No reply.

Months passed. I wrote a second letter to Jake, repeating that I appreciated his help in setting up the meeting but that I would reluctantly have to take my proposal elsewhere if I couldn't get any response from Margaret's office.

No reply.

The following June, almost a year after our meeting, I faxed her to ask if I could get her take on my proposal from the previous summer, and whether I should be aware of any circumstances that had kept her from responding to all my previous messages.

No reply.

I never heard from Margaret again.

One might well ask what motivates people like this to act so rudely and so callously for no apparent reason. Wouldn't it have been easier to just say, 'We're not interested, thank you'? Maybe not responding was a simple demonstration of power.

I figured that the only explanation for Margaret's behavior was Jake's phone call to her, directing her to meet with me; perhaps it so damaged her sense of self-importance that she couldn't bring herself to cooperate. If it had been her idea from the start, or if I had contacted her before anyone else in the building, maybe things would have turned out differently.

CHAPTER TWENTY-SIX

* * *

After finally giving up on trying to speak to Margaret, I turned my attention to the CEO of the Warner Music Group, whom we'll call 'Dave.' At the time, he was in charge of my three favorite labels—Warner Bros, Elektra, and Atlantic. I knew a lot of people at these labels, and I loved the Time Warner organization. Mo Ostin had offered me a post at Warner Bros in 1980, which I had turned down, and I'd often thought about how things might have been if I had said yes and gone over to the wonderful Warner Bros Records headquarters in Burbank. Even so, I did remain close to the Warner Music Group and would visit 75 Rockefeller Plaza each time I came to New York.

Back in the 80s, I had spent some quality time with Dave at Atlantic. He had an Asteroids arcade game in his office, and I'd show him tricks I picked up while playing the game in various recording studio lounges.

I figured he and I were solid. Right? Wrong.

I made an appointment with him in November of 1994 at the Atlantic office in LA, but then his New York secretary called me the day before the meeting and canceled. We rescheduled the meeting for January. Dave's secretary called to cancel that one as well.

We rescheduled a second time for March, and when I arrived at the Atlantic office I was told that Dave was unavailable. I was pretty amazed at this third consecutive cancellation, but I salvaged the hour by accepting an invitation from the talented Atlantic A&R man Jason Flom to buy me lunch at the Peninsula Hotel. Imagine my surprise when I saw Dave having lunch two tables away with two other Atlantic executives. We said a brief hello in passing, and he offered no apology.

After further failed attempts to set up a meeting on the phone, I sent Dave a fax, telling him I'd been trying to get fifteen minutes of his time for half a year, and would very much appreciate it if we could set something up on either coast.

No reply.

In May, I traveled to New York, and on my first day in the city I phoned Dave's office. He was there, I was told, but 'unable to speak to me.' On Tuesday morning, I was at the Warner Music Group executive offices for an appointment with the lovely and courteous attorney Ina Meibach, and Dave happened to walk right by. How lucky for me. I stood up and said hello and asked if I could have ten minutes of his time at any point that week.

'How's tomorrow morning at eleven?' he replied. 'Is that good for you?'

'I'll make it good,' I said. 'Thanks.' Finally, after more than six months of frustration and at least fifteen phone calls, I'd be able to get a good indication of the direction my musical career might take.

I arrived at Dave's office the next morning at five minutes to eleven. Dave never came in that day. I never had an explanation or an apology. No phone call from his office, no attempt to reschedule, not a word. Did this happen in other industries? Arrogance is often evident in executive suites, but this kind of behavior can only be classified as vengeance. I still haven't figured out what it was that I did to make him go that far out of his way to show me how much more powerful he was than me. Had I slandered him in the press? Sent him a dead flounder wrapped in the pages of *Billboard*?

Another possible target, and another Warner Group imprint, was Elektra Records, one of my favorite labels. I had done five records for Elektra, four of which were multi-platinum. I had been a senior VP of A&R and had left the label with a production deal. But now the label was headed by a woman we'll call 'Sara,' who was, coincidentally, appointed by Dave . . .

I sent Sara my proposal packet, and two weeks later I spoke to her longtime assistant, who set up an appointment for me with Sara for later that month. Now we were getting somewhere, it seemed. Or not. Not surprisingly, the assistant canceled two days before the meeting.

'Sara doesn't have time to see you.'

Well, at least she was direct.

I made various other phone calls over the coming weeks, but to no avail. At one point, a date in April looked like it might be good for a meeting, as long as Sara didn't have jury duty that day. Naturally, I never did hear from her. She must have learned her code of ethics from Dave or Margaret.

* * *

The man in charge of the Polygram labels—we'll call him 'Edward'—was another person I felt it was important to see. I had met him when I was at Epic Records, and he always seemed friendly and relaxed. I didn't think it would be too difficult to get a few minutes with him, so I sent him my proposal package and began calling his office to request a meeting. After several calls, his secretary told me, 'Oh, I don't think he'll want to meet with you.'

I respectfully requested that I'd like to hear this from the boss himself, so she suggested that I might want to fax him. Which I did.

No reply.

After fourteen phone calls and six faxes, I was no closer to my ten minutes with Edward than I had been when I first called three months earlier. But then, as luck would have it, I was in the building on another appointment, and miraculously I ran into him on the elevator. He didn't apologize for not returning umpteen phone calls and faxes. Instead, he said he'd have the president of Island Records call me when he was in LA for Don Henley's wedding later in May...

Lucky me. I had originally contacted this guy, who we'll call 'Jack,' at the suggestion of a good friend of his, A&R man John Kalodner.

John was a friend and a straight shooter who had been helpful to me in the past, so I figured if he was friends with this guy, maybe I could avoid the ritual bullshit I'd had to wade through with all these other people.

No such luck.

After six months, I was finally able to secure a meeting with Jack. Despite his apparent insensitivity to phone calls, he seemed like a pleasant and sincere man, and I could see why John liked him. We had a nice chat; he introduced me to some of the other people at Island Records, and he concluded the meeting by saying that he thought I should have a meeting with Chris Blackwell, the CEO and founder of Island Records.

This, of course, never came to pass.

CHAPTER TWENTY-SEVEN

THE ROCK STAR AND THE INNKEEPER

After EMI Capitol Entertainment Properties folded and my contract was paid off, I got a phone call from Budd Carr, a very successful film music supervisor who had hundreds of credits on big films and who knew most of the studio executives, producers, and directors of note. Budd had managed Kansas ('Dust In The Wind') when they were with Epic back in the 70s and had now been hired to supervise the music for *Rock Star*, a big-budget film starring Jennifer Aniston and Mark Wahlberg. It was set in the 80s, so Budd thought I'd be a natural to produce the original music for the film.

Rock Star is based on a true story about a young Pittsburgh singer named Tim 'Ripper' Owens, who fronted a Judas Priest tribute band. When Judas Priest's original singer, Rob Halford, was fired, Owens was hired as his replacement. It was a real-life heavy-metal Cinderella story. The screenplay featured two bands—Judas Priest, called Steel Dragon in the film, and the tribute band, Blood Pollution—and each would be playing the same songs throughout the film. I had to make Steel Dragon sound as if they'd been together for ten years; Blood Pollution, playing the same songs note-for-note, needed to sound just a little younger, newer, and not quite as good as their idols.

In a regular album project for a record label, the producer runs the show. But when you're the music producer for a film, you're definitely not the one in control. You and the musicians can hang out in the studio for up to twelve hours a day (sometimes more, if required) and wait for the assistant director or music editor to phone in musical orders directly from the set. We'd deliver a finished song for them to roll film to, and then the director would decide to make a change in the action; we'd get a phone call to say they needed the lead guitar break to be thirteen seconds shorter, or the song to come to a dead stop instead of a fade—and they needed it by noon tomorrow.

I'd be sitting behind the console, thinking back to the night before, when we were up mixing the song until 2am, and in my mind all I could hear was Elvis.

'Thank you. Thank you very much.'

Budd and I assembled the two bands for the film. For Steel Dragon, he managed to get Zakk Wylde and Jason Bonham. Zakk had been Ozzy Osbourne's lead guitarist for years, and Jason was the son of the one and only Zeppelin drummer, John Bonham. Jason was a solid rock drummer and Zakk was a lightning-fast guitar shredder. I realized that keeping these two gentlemen focused and working together would probably not be an easy task, so I suggested to Budd that we also hire Jeff Pilson, who was Dokken's bass player when I worked with them in the early 80s. Jeff was a very good musician and a level-headed team player who could act as the group leader and help to keep the others focused.

One evening, Jason stumbled into the control room while Zakk was recording a guitar solo. Jason had obviously had a few, and he playfully threw his arms around Zakk, trying to give him a kiss on the cheek. Alarmed, Zakk grabbed Jason, yanked him clean off the floor, and threw him on the couch. We're talking about a two-hundred-pound man here.

Before filming began, there was a cocktail party to kick off the project, so that the cast and crew might get together and enjoy a little personal contact. Jennifer Aniston brought Brad Pitt along. I was chatting with a couple of cameramen when Jennifer walked over to us with Brad. I introduced myself and told Brad that I was the music producer for the film.

'Hi, I'm Brad,' he said.

'Nice to meet you,' I replied, and then, in a moment of silliness, I asked, 'So what do you do, Brad?' It was one of my better lines, but unfortunately, he didn't hear it above the noise of the party.

I never had an opportunity to spend even a few seconds with Jennifer Aniston during the filming, but I did get to spend some time with Mark Wahlberg. We chatted about Boston and demonstrated our best Boston accents. I explained that only a handful of actors had ever done it properly. You don't just drop the *r* on the end of the word, but instead, you defer it to the beginning of the next word. It's not '*I took my cah and I brought it to the shop*'; it's '*I took my cah rand I brought it to the shop.*' Similarly, '*law offices*' becomes '*lah roffices.*'

Mark was soft-spoken and modest, and definitely not a Hollywood type. He seemed to be a very serious actor, too, and stayed in character when he was off the set. He went out with the guys in the movie band to metal clubs at night to observe the lifestyle and become a credible character. He and I talked about his troubled upbringing, and he told me that he went to church every single day. I think he did this because he knew his childhood sins could have easily earned him some jail time, but because he decided to start doing the right thing, he turned out to be one very successful guy.

In the film, the two band's lead singers both have huge vocal ranges and reach extraordinarily high notes. A few years earlier, I had produced a band called Steelheart, whose singer, Michael Matijevic, had a stratospheric voice. He and session singer Jeff Scott Soto provided the vocals for the soundtrack.

Rock Star was a good final recording project for me. It provided me with an important role in the making of a major motion picture and gave me the opportunity to see how a film was made day-to-day, and how the huge crew operated. The film's director, Stephen Herek, even let me be an extra in the hotel lobby scene. In my international cinematic debut, I'm visible for at least three or four seconds. Despite my stunning and impactful onscreen presence, however, I was never offered another acting job.

* * *

When the movie project was finished, I didn't have any producing offers that appealed to me. I'd complain to my golf buddy Tom Kelly about my failure to find something meaningful to do, or to get the kind of big-name producing gigs I used to get—or about my golf game.

One day, Tom told me he had a book I should read, and the next time we met, he gave me a small volume titled *Who Moved My Cheese?* I sat down in our bedroom and read the book in under an hour the next day.

At first glance, *Who Moved My Cheese?* appears to be a children's book about a couple of mice, but it's actually a how-to book about dealing with unanticipated change. It tells the story of two mice who navigate a maze every day in order to eat the cheese. One day, the cheese isn't in its usual spot; the first mouse urges the other mouse to help him search the maze for the cheese, but the second mouse refuses, angrily declaring that he won't budge until he finds out who is responsible for this. The first mouse goes off to find the cheese, scribbling messages on the walls of the maze as he goes. One of them urges the angry mouse to smell the cheese frequently, so he knows when it's getting old.

The angry mouse never finds the cheese—he just remains where he was, and he fumes. The lesson? Whatever the cheese represents—your job, your income, your satisfaction—when you can no longer find it, or if someone or something removes it, just roll with the changes. Don't sit there and stamp your foot; adapt, adopt a new attitude, adjust, and move on.

After considering the book's message for a few minutes, I concluded that I should fly back to New England and find a nice place that we could convert into a 'luxury B&B'—an oxymoron at the time. Back then, B&Bs all shared a certain spartan quality—part of their charm was an absence of conveniences or technology. You were lucky if there was an AM radio in your room. I thought it was a good time to create an inn with three-room suites, strong Wi-Fi, big-screen TVs, CD players, and a big tasty breakfast.

I scheduled appointments with realtors in Brattleboro and Bennington in Vermont, and in Williamstown, Pittsfield, Northampton, Stockbridge, North Adams, Great Barrington, and Lenox in Massachusetts—all part of the Berkshires region. Most of the places I was shown were shabby and unsuitable—even with extensive renovation.

Lenox was my last stop. I was staying with friends in Williamstown, and on the day of my Lenox appointments, it was sleeting hard. I left early because of the weather and arrived with time to spare. I bought a cup of coffee in the village and chose a road to cruise down to kill time until I met the broker.

A couple of miles down the road, I came upon a magnificent farm, built in 1890, with a main house, a cottage, an abandoned schoolhouse, and an enormous barn. With a little investigation, I learned that although it was in a residential zone, it had a special permit allowing it to operate as a B&B. The next morning, my broker and I went to look at it. As soon as I walked in the door, I saw that this was the place. Suky flew out to see it, and within five short months, we had sold our homes in both LA and Nantucket and were living in Lenox, Massachusetts.

We renovated for a year before opening the doors on July 4th weekend in 2001 to our first guest, Linda Ronstadt, along with her agent Shelly Schultz and her producer/manager, John Boylan. Linda was performing at Tanglewood that weekend (a half-mile walk from the house) and we were invited to the show, with backstage access. The experience was a little bittersweet for me—I had become a small-town innkeeper, but I was still viewing the record business in my rearview mirror. Over time, however, Suky and I developed the B&B into an award-winning vacation and wedding destination; we were delighted to host the occasional musical or theater or political celebrity, we loved the weddings, we established friendships with our regulars, and we felt very much at home on our ten-acre gentleman's farm.

After twenty years, we sold it, moved down the road a mile, and have been blissfully retired for a couple of years.

CHAPTER TWENTY-EIGHT

CRITICAL THOUGHTS, CRITICAL VALUES

If a piece of music moves you, then it's good music. Period. If the music turns you on, it's effective. Similarly, if you like the taste of what you're eating, then regardless of the quality of the chef, to you it's good food. It's the same with music. While a song or album may not be a critical success, if it moves you, you consider it good music. It's neither fair nor productive for a 'critic' to judge a piece of music merely by his or her personal standards.

Most music critics have agendas: Robert Hilburn wrote for the *Los Angeles Times* during the 70s, when I was cranking out hard-rock records and lots of people were buying them. You could almost feel his frustration as he wrote over and over about how vapid and useless hard rock was while he gushed enthusiastically—and almost exclusively—over new-wave and punk bands.

Elsewhere, the music critic Richard Goldstein once wrote, 'For all its diversity, *Sgt Pepper* is a philosophical whole, presenting a certain attitude toward identity and style. Both are mutable and self-generated—the essence of the hippie worldview.'

Come again? Do these words have anything at all to do with the music on *Sgt Pepper* or how it affects you? Do 'She's Leaving Home,' 'With A Little Help From My Friends,' 'When I'm 64,' or 'Good Morning Good Morning' really 'present a certain attitude toward identity and style'? And, more importantly, does this provide me with even a single clue as to whether I'd like the album or not?

In 2015, *Rolling Stone* magazine decided that Johnny Winter was the sixty-third greatest guitarist of all time. What guitar fan was assigned the task of carefully listing the best to the worst in specific numerical order? And what if the writer who was charged with deciding exactly who ranked just above and just below Johnny preferred the dobro or the acoustic guitar to the Fender Stratocaster or the Les Paul? And who determined that Joe Walsh was only number fifty-four? My taste places him in the top ten; the magazine admittedly did consult a panel of guitar players, but I believe they also factored in the musical taste of a panel of critics. If I had been selected for that panel, Joe would have been placed in a significantly higher spot. And if I had been selected for that panel, the person who selected me for the panel would apparently have respected my taste in guitar players.

It's fine to have an opinion, to share it with friends, to discuss the merits of individual musicians—but to declare yourself the arbiter of taste by publishing what you declare is a definitive pecking order is bogus.

Similarly, one producer might turn out a record that sounds quite different from one that another producer would make with the very same artist. It's all about the producer's personal approach and his interpretation of the songs.

I listen to the Foo Fighters song 'End Over End' frequently, because it's on my workout playlist, but I had to hear it several times before I noticed a couple of vocal harmony lines in the chorus. At first, they're barely audible; while their volume seems to increase slightly with each chorus, my guess is that Dave Grohl wanted to keep them low so that the song retained its edge and didn't come across as too 'pop.'

If I had produced the song, I would have brought these harmony lines up—just a bit lower in volume than the lead vocal. This would have resulted in a much more obvious and traditional three-part harmony, and it would have given the song a more 'pop' sound. I would have done this because I'm a sucker for choral harmonies—and, who knows, maybe it would have earned the song more airplay. Mr. Grohl may have done what he did to keep the song from sounding like 'corporate rock.'

For a song to touch your emotions—regardless of its success in the marketplace—it should be well written, well performed, effectively arranged, and well mixed. If any one of those elements is absent, the chances of it being a powerful piece of music are certainly reduced.

When a producer or a recording engineer listens to music, he listens in a way that's different from the way an average listener does—probably in the same way a movie director views a movie. I notice if something is too muddy or too bright, or if the track could benefit from some percussion, or if a verse could improve with a nice string arrangement, or maybe with a Hammond B3 organ, and so on.

There aren't many songs I've heard that I'd leave exactly as they were produced. Most of the time there's something that I feel could be improved—an individual performance, an arrangement, or the mix itself. And other producers and engineers likely feel the same way about my productions. To each his own.

* * *

After I'd been gone from the music business for about a decade, I was cruising the internet one day and came across an interesting site called Popdose.com. A contributor to the site had written a piece that was allegedly about Mötley Crüe, but which was actually a scathing indictment of 'producer Tom Werman ... a guy with a hard-rock résumé and a soft-rock mind.'

'Bossy, egotistical, and either in denial or oblivious to the damage his attitude has caused him,' the writer wrote, 'Werman was known for his dogmatism in the studio, preferring to force slick arrangements on bands whose type of music would seem to call for something louder and rougher.'

Blindsided and defensive, I responded to the piece, which had portrayed me as a dictatorial, self-absorbed musical hack. The site's editor, Jeff Giles, asked if I'd be interested in writing a rebuttal to be posted on the site, which I did—and which is still there on the site, should you want to read it.

Following the receipt of this response, Jeff asked if I would write a series. I agreed, and over time I contributed eighteen installments on different aspects of a career in recording. I enjoyed the process so much that I decided to write this book.

* * *

Music fans all have their favorite players. In rock'n'roll, few would deny that Paul McCartney, John Entwistle, Timothy Schmitt, or John McVie are excellent bass players, or that Mick Fleetwood, Keith Carlock, Ringo Starr, Keith Moon, or Bun E. Carlos are excellent drummers, but consider how each one serves his band.

Charlie Watts's drumming never takes center stage, but it anchors the song with steady time and minimal fills. Compare this to the drumming of Keith Moon, who sometimes sounds like he's playing one continuous drum solo for the entire length of a song. But The Who simply wouldn't have been The Who—or the Stones the Stones—without Keith Moon's overplaying or Charlie Watts's minimalism.

Mick Fleetwood's drumming felt so natural for Fleetwood Mac's songs that each tune could have been written on and for the drums. Anyone who's ever seen Steely Dan live with Keith Carlock on drums might think he's the very best of them all—how can a drummer play with the precise meter of a metronome and still have such great feel? Consider Bun E. Carlos, Tommy Lee, or Don Henley—all great drummers, but ill-fitted for any band other than the ones each of them helped to make famous.

What makes Paul McCartney the best bass player I've ever heard? He doesn't reel off bass lines that are as intricate as John Entwistle's, but to me, the notes he plays are always precisely what the song needs. His bass lines are melodic and effortless, and the sequences of notes he plays are surprising and unexpected. His playing on The Beatles' 'Something' is a fascinating example.

Timothy B. Schmitt of the Eagles is a supportive player who provides a minimal role without ever grabbing the spotlight. He plays what's needed, wedded to Don Henley's kick drum. The same can be said of Sting, who provides good, thoughtful support for a song but doesn't typically play anything as involved or ornate as McCartney does.

Compare the guitar playing of Joe Walsh to that of Keith Richards. Keith's guitar playing relies heavily on feel and is certainly not precise. Onstage, he approaches notes, sometimes landing on them, sometimes grazing them, and occasionally missing them altogether. By contrast, guitarists like Joe Walsh, Mark Knopfler, Jeff Beck, Skunk Baxter, Rick Derringer, John Mayer, or Vince Gill are precision players who hit every note they intend to hit—they hit those notes dead center, and, if they bend a note, they don't let go until they've arrived at the exact pitch they intended. But they can do this with great feel, as well. Precision doesn't preclude a soulful performance. Walsh's guitar work with the Eagles is as engaging as his playing in The James Gang. He's one of the most instantly identifiable guitar players in rock'n'roll.

George Harrison rarely failed to hit every note on the head and managed to play parts that sounded natural to every Beatles song. Pete Townshend's playing is powerful, emotional, and aggressive. He's a more effective rhythm player than he is a lead guitarist, and certainly it's his right hand that established The Who's musical signature, rather than his left.

In The Rolling Stones' 'Brown Sugar,' Keith introduces a couple of catchy guitar licks before the first verse even arrives. He adds a third figure in the chorus. These separate guitar lines fit together perfectly. It may be that he came up with all three licks at one sitting, and just figured out a way to use them all. Maybe not. Either way, I think he composed the catchiest, most infectious guitar riffs in all of rock'n'roll.

Lyndsey Buckingham played a variety of stringed instruments on Fleetwood Mac's *Rumours* album, which in my opinion, aside from The Beatles and the Stones, is the top album in the 'bang for your buck' category. Many of his guitar parts sounded a little wacky, and if you listen to them in isolation they may not make a lot of musical sense; but again, they serve the songs perfectly. His playing was unorthodox and unique, and his sometimes schizophrenic style probably wouldn't have worked so well with any other group.

Mick Fleetwood plays a drum fill right through a musical rest in 'Yesterday's Gone,' completing the fill in the middle of the next vocal line. Keith Moon aside, drummers don't usually do this. But Fleetwood played what he felt like playing at the moment. He didn't confine himself to a set pattern, especially when it came to fills or turnarounds. Don Henley, whom few people regard first and foremost as a drummer, played straightforward and understated drum parts, anchoring the track and staying out of the way—just like Tim Schmitt, the other half of the Eagle's precise rhythm section.

Remember that a drummer is playing four different rhythmic patterns with four separate limbs; Henley still manages to deliver an effortless, soulful vocal during live performances while playing drums at the same time. This is not a simple feat. Keith Moon played anything but a pattern. At times, he seemed to improvise an entire song. His simplest drum fill was about as busy as Henley's most complex drum fill. Rather than playing a consistent rhythm, he strung together fill after fill, but the result was right for the song.

On the negative side, I may be one of few listeners to consider the guitar solos in Foreigner's 'Hot Blooded' and Eric Clapton's 'Layla' to be subpar. Many fans will say it's blasphemous to label anything Duane Allman ever played as such, but to my ears, the slide guitar solo in 'Layla' suffers from below-average composition and pretty poor execution. I can't imagine any high-fives following a control room playback of that particular performance. And, compared to most of his other guitar performances, Mick Jones's guitar solo on 'Hot Blooded'—I'm assuming he was the one who played it—is sloppy, and at the end, it just sounds as if he broke a few strings.

If you're a fan of lead guitar, you'll love George Lynch's lead break on Dokken's 'Tooth & Nail,' or the stunning guitar solo that ends Hendrix's 'Axis Bold As Love,' or just about all of Billy Gibbons's lead work on ZZ Top's *Eliminator* LP, or the last minute of Tom Petty's 'Runnin' Down A Dream,' or anything Joe Walsh ever played…

Many early Rolling Stones songs had effective—but not necessarily obvious—percussion. The mention of 'Sympathy For The Devil' or 'Gimme Shelter'—or, for that matter, the name of the band—certainly doesn't bring to mind tambourines or shakers or guiros, but there are few early Stones songs without some very audible driving percussion: the hand-claps in 'Gimme Shelter,' the guiro that runs through the first three quarters of the song; the shaker in 'You Can't Always Get What You Want,' joined by a tambourine for the last minute of the song; the essential tambourine in 'Paint It Black'; or the castanets in the intro and the shakers after the lead break in 'Brown Sugar.'

* * *

A hit song will almost always have a balanced and compelling arrangement; a good example of a well-arranged (and well-played) song is Bruce Hornsby's 'Every Little Kiss,' or maybe Gerry Rafferty's 'Baker

Street.' The lead guitar 'fills' in the latter are well composed, perfectly executed, and placed in just the right spots—namely, between vocal lines.

The interplay between Hornsby's piano and the lead guitar on 'Across The River'—one panned to the right, the other to the left—is perfectly balanced. The arrangement of this song is noteworthy.

Another example of a song that's well written, well played, well arranged, well recorded, and well produced is Phil Collins's 'Take Me Home.' The rhythmic figure and the keyboard part at the song's opening comprise the entire platform of the tune and are played nonstop from the very start to the very last note of the song. It's mesmerizing.

Some recordings are just well conceived and well executed all around. A good producer will have a lot to do with the arranging (not necessarily the playing and singing), providing guidance to the artist, and identifying the best performances.

I have always responded strongly to certain songs by other artists that were hits during my years in the studio. They inspired me, and each of them had most of the elements that I considered essential to a good production. Here are a few in particular:

BILLY IDOL, 'DON'T NEED A GUN': You can hear every instrument clearly, all the time, and both producer Keith Forsey's conga playing and Steve Stevens's pyrotechnic guitar playing are outstanding.

TOTO, 'ROSANNA': This song has a dynamic range and feelings that span the emotional distance between sacred and explosive. Steve Lukather's guitar work is stunning.

THE ROLLING STONES, 'STREET FIGHTING MAN': A powerful song from beginning to end. Keith's rhythm acoustic guitar playing and Bill Wyman's bass are terrific.

EAGLES, 'HOTEL CALIFORNIA': A guitar tour-de-force, with well-conceived, distinctive, nicely placed guitar fills that never step on the colorful lyrics—and, although it's six and a half minutes long, when it's over, you still haven't heard enough.

EAGLES, 'TAKE IT EASY': A loping, smooth, forward-moving feel with a classic, well-played snare/kick drum pattern—and a great banjo! It makes you drive faster.

THE PRODIGY, 'FUNKY SHIT': Aside from a questionable title, this song has sounds you never heard before and may never hear again. Hardly any of them is identifiable. There was clearly an effort here to record sounds that were obviously machine-made, sharp-edged, aggressive, and brand new to the listener. They all work together, and the song's energy ebbs and flows—it's a somewhat exhausting listening experience.

THE POINTER SISTERS, 'I'M SO EXCITED,' 'NEUTRON DANCE': There are so many things going on here—several different rhythms, all integrated into one funky steamroller of a song, and so energetic and positive. Both of these songs are great Richard Perry productions.

THE CARPENTERS, 'GOODBYE TO LOVE': This one has always moved me. Considering how Karen Carpenter brought about her own demise, the lyrics (written by her brother Richard and Richard Bettis) are so meaningful and so very sad, and Tony Peluso's guitar work is wonderful.

SEAL, 'CRAZY': There are so many different instruments and rhythms in this song—lots of subtle percussion (for example, the shaker on the right side during the chorus) and an insistent, forward-moving groove created by using so many different elements that slide along on a greased Brazilian-flavored keyboard bed. Much of the song features just one lead vocal and only one harmony vocal. There are few audible backing vocals in the choruses—a rare thing indeed. The first verse opens with a pronounced keyboard 'clang'—a nice exclamation point for the first verse—but you never hear that sound again. This tune is four and a half minutes long, but it isn't boring or repetitive. Even though the music seems computer-generated, it feels warm and organic, not cold or mechanical. What are those instruments? Instead of using obviously computerized sounds, producer Trevor Horn uses sounds that could have been generated by real people playing real instruments. Everything is precisely placed, recorded, and mixed at just the right level. The number of separate instruments is impressive, with many of them appearing only once in the song. To me, this is a nearly perfectly produced record.

AFTERWORD

MAN VS. MACHINE

When Charlie Watts slows down a touch after the drums come in for the first time on 'Street Fighting Man,' you can visualize him sitting at the drum kit as he does so. There's a wonderful version of 'Midnight Rambler' on the *Get Yer Ya-Ya's Out* album, recorded live at Madison Square Garden in 1968, when Bill Wyman seems to introduce the bass one measure too early at the start of the song; then, in the breakdown in the middle of the song, you can hear the snares on Charlie Watts's snare drum rattling from the vibrations of Wyman's bass. These elements allow the listener to visualize the live performance by the band. They're *real* musical moments—the kind that just don't exist on computer-perfected twenty-first-century recordings.

When we made records in the last century, we *listened* to the music. Now, engineers and producers rely on a computer screen, and they *look at* the music. Almost everything today comes from the computer. Perfection reigns. If there are actual live studio performances, producers and engineers can use a myriad of devices to correct sharp and flat vocals, or perhaps variations in the meter of the drums. In fact, there are devices to make every single aspect of a recording absolutely perfect. But repetition and sameness can cause one to tire of a song quickly.

A young friend introduced me to house music recently, and I loved a few songs, which I put on my gym workout playlist. Initially, I found them stimulating, but their appeal wore off after a few weeks. With repeated plays, I came to hear that every musical figure or element in the song was used multiple times. This may explain why today's young music listeners are surprisingly familiar with the music of the 70s and 80s. That music feels more human, and one can hear the variations, imperfections, and mistakes. Again, this lets the listener visualize a live performance. With today's music, all the listener can visualize is the computer, the screen, and the keyboard that generates all the sampled sounds.

In the 70s and 80s, we frequently used 'click tracks'—a metronome in the drummer's headphones. Some drummers needed to play to the click track right through the song, but the good ones would use the click track simply to establish the meter; once they were locked in and playing in time with the click, I could gradually fade it out of his headphones.

The earliest uses of computerized sounds in rock music, such as The Who's 'Won't Get Fooled Again' or 'Baba O'Riley,' established an insistent pulse, but everything else in the song was organic, and played by real people. The machine established a core, and all the musicians locked into that pulse.

In the mid-80s, producers began to use samples (as on Yes's 'Owner Of A Lonely Heart,' or, in my case, Mötley Crüe's 'Wild Side'). They would take sections or riffs from a song and use them in their own songs. They'd be digitally recorded, then triggered by a keyboard or a computer.

In the earlier days of hit-making, some record producers would organize their favorite professional musicians into a studio unit they'd use to provide the music for many or most of their acts. In the 60s, the "Wrecking Crew (Hal Blaine, Leon Russell, Glen Campbell, et al.) worked frequently for Phil Spector when he made hits for The Crystals, The Ronettes, The Righteous Brothers, and many more. Philadelphia's MFSB (mother, father, sister, brother) worked with the fine production team of Kenny Gamble and Leon Huff at Sigma Sound Studios, recording tracks for acts like The O'Jays and Harold Melvin & The Blue Notes. The Muscle Shoals Rhythm Section, out of Muscle Shoals

Sound in Alabama, provided the music for stars ranging from Rod Stewart and Glenn Frey to Paul Simon and Joe Cocker. Producers also provided constant studio work for noted players like Waddy Wachtel, Danny Kortchmar, Russ Kunkel, Lee Sklar, Hal Blaine, Jim Gordon, and David Foster—all of whose performances can be heard on dozens of hit records.

After the digital revolution, things were different. Asked recently who of today's professional studio musicians he would choose to succeed these fabled session men, producer Rick Rubin answered frankly, 'I'm not sure. You really don't need bands anymore.' Sad but true.

I have a four-hour playlist on my phone, and I still love listening to it and revisiting my rock'n'roll life—a time when we made records that lived and breathed, warts and all. Looking back, and loving what I hear, I've come to understand why times gone by are called the *good* old days.

APPENDIX ONE SELECT DISCOGRAPHY

BABYLON A.D.
Nothing Sacred (Arista, 1992)

JEFF BECK
Live With Jan Hammer (Epic, 1977) gold

BLUE ÖYSTER CULT
Mirrors (Columbia, 1979)

BROWNSVILLE
Air Special (Atlantic, 1978)

BOY MEETS GIRL
Boy Meets Girl (A&M, 1985)

THE B'ZZ
Get Up (Epic, 1982)

CHEAP TRICK
In Color (Epic, 1977) platinum
Heaven Tonight (Epic, 1978) platinum
Dream Police (Epic, 1979) platinum

DOKKEN
Tooth & Nail (Elektra, 1984) platinum

LITA FORD
Dangerous Curves (RCA, 1991)

FOUR-IN-LEGION
Four-In-Legion (CBS, 1984)

HASH
Hash (Elektra, 1993)

HAWKS
Hawks (Columbia, 1981)

HOLLAND
Little Monsters (Atlantic, 1985)

JASON & THE SCORCHERS
Still Standing (EMI, 1986)

JUNKYARD
Junkyard (Geffen, 1989)

KIX
Blow My Fuse (Atlantic, 1988) platinum
Hot Wire (Atlantic, 1991) gold

KROKUS
Change Of Address (Arista, 1986)

LA GUNS
Cocked & Loaded (Polygram, 1989) platinum

LOVE HATE
Blackout In The Red Room (Columbia, 1990)

MCQUEEN STREET
McQueen Street (SBK, 1991)

MOLLY HATCHET
Molly Hatchet (Epic, 1978) 2x platinum
Flirtin' With Disaster (Epic, 1979) 2x platinum
Beatin' The Odds (Epic, 1980) platinum
Take No Prisoners (Epic, 1981) gold
No Guts, No Glory (Epic, 1983) gold

MÖTLEY CRÜE
Shout At The Devil (Elektra, 1983) 3x platinum
Theater Of Pain (Elektra, 1985) 3x platinum
Girls, Girls, Girls (Elektra, 1987) 3x platinum

MOTHER'S FINEST
Mother's Finest (Epic, 1976)
Another Mother Further (Epic, 1977)

GARY MYRICK & THE FIGURES
She Talks In Stereo (Epic, 1980)

TED NUGENT
Ted Nugent (Epic, 1975) 2x platinum
Free For All (Epic, 1976) 2x platinum
Cat Scratch Fever (Epic, 1977) 3x platinum
Double Live Gonzo (Epic, 1978) 3x platinum
Weekend Warriors (Epic, 1978) 2x platinum

OFF BROADWAY
On (Atlantic, 1979)

PARIAH
To Mock A Killingbird (Geffen, 1993)

POISON
Open Up And Say... Ahh! (Capitol, 1988) 5x platinum

THE PRODUCERS
The Producers (Portrait, 1981)
You Make The Heat (Portrait, 1982)

ROCK STAR
Original Soundtrack (Atlantic, 2001)

STRANGER
Stranger (Epic, 1982)

STRYPER
Against The Law (Enigma, 1990)

TWISTED SISTER
Stay Hungry (Atlantic, 1984) 5x platinum

APPENDIX TWO GREATEST HITS & MISSES

When Suky and I opened our B&B, I knew it would be the end of my career in the record business. It was a bittersweet moment—a combination of nostalgia and anticipation—and I thought it would be nice to have something to permanently close out my thirty years of music.

I decided to create a two-CD gift set for my friends and family titled *Tom Werman's Greatest Hits & Greatest Misses*, with all the familiar hit songs on one disc and my favorite lesser-heard productions on the other—all the songs I felt should have been hits. They're every bit as good as—or even better than—the hits.

THE HITS
'Girls, Girls, Girls,' Mötley Crüe
'Surrender,' Cheap Trick
'I Want You To Want Me,' Cheap Trick
'Cat Scratch Fever,' Ted Nugent
'We're Not Gonna Take It,' Twisted Sister
'Every Rose Has Its Thorn,' Poison
'Dream Police,' Cheap Trick
'It's All Over Now,' Molly Hatchet
'Flirtin' With Disaster,' Molly Hatchet
'Home Sweet Home,' Motley Crue
'She Talks In Stereo,' Gary Myrick & The Figures
'Hey Baby,' Ted Nugent
'Shout At The Devil,' Motley Crue
'A Shot Of Poison,' Lita Ford
'Don't Close Your Eyes,' KIX
'Stranglehold,' Ted Nugent

THE MISSES
'What's He Got?,' The Producers
'Mickey's Monkey,' Mother's Finest
'Who Do You Love?,' Brownsville
'Don't Tell Me,' Boy Meets Girl
'Why Do You Think They Call It Dope?,' Love Hate
'Blinded,' Glass Tiger
'Get Up, Get Angry,' The B'zz
'Let Me In,' Hawks
'School's Out,' Krokus
'Truth Gonna Set You Free,' Mother's Finest
'Admiral's Mutiny,' Hawks
'Rip & Tear,' LA Guns
'Life Of Crime,' The Producers
'Do You Know How To Rock?,' Pariah
'Auf Wiedersehen,' Cheap Trick
'Change The World,' Graveyard Train
'Blue Wind' (live), Jeff Beck

APPENDIX THREE THE PMRC LETTER

One day in December 1985, two men—Raymond Belknap, 18, and James Vance, 20—spent six hours drinking, smoking marijuana and listening to Judas Priest's *Stained Class* album, after which each man took a shotgun and shot himself. Belknap died instantly but Vance lived, sustaining serious injuries that left him disfigured; he died three years later.

Before his death, Vance and his parents sued the band and their label at the time, CBS Records, for $6.2 million in damages. They claimed that Judas Priest had hidden subliminal messages like 'try suicide,' 'do it,' and 'let's be dead' in their cover of Spooky Tooth's 'Better By You, Better Than Me,' influencing Vance and Belknap to form a suicide pact. The suit went to trial in July, 1990, and the prosecution played the song forward, backward, and sped up in an attempt to prove the group had brainwashed these two young men into killing themselves.

This prompted me to write the following letter to *Music Exchange*, as published in their issue dated February 18–March 3, 1991:

When I first heard of the Judas Priest lawsuit, brought by the parents of a boy who killed himself, I felt badly for the anguished couple, although at that time I did feel that the suit was without merit (and for a minute, relieved that it wasn't one of my records that was on the poor teenager's turntable). But it was just this thought—that it might have been a Mötley Crüe album, or a Twisted Sister album, or even a Cheap Trick record (they dealt with suicide in a song called 'Auf Weidersehen') that suggested to me the absurdity of the entire suit, which I now feel is at best regrettable, and at worst morally bankrupt. Since then, there has been considerable discussion in the various media concerning the 'influence' which rock music has on its listeners (our children).

In a society which scolds its children for listening to 'explicit' lyrics, but which condones their watching a collection of capital crimes and beatings nightly on network TV, it seems that our priorities are seriously confused; when my nine-year-old son may not view a movie in which a breast is bared (rated R), but can see a film with any number of murders (rated PG), one must ask some very basic questions. Why am I cautioned by stickers informing me that the lyrics of a song may deal with sex when 'responsible' corporate sponsors spend hundreds of millions on television scripts which routinely, graphically and in slow motion depict an endless stream of humans killing other humans? Catch my drift? And yet we have allowed the fundamentalist few, through our silence and sloth, to back us into a corner, where we can seriously question our own values as an industry. Judging by these legislated standards, ours is simply a society which fears sex, but embraces violence.

What can those of us who help to create the music say to any parent who has suffered the loss of a child by suicide? The pain of the parents must be almost unbearable. But after the sincerest words of condolence and sympathy have been spoken, and after the tears have been shed, certain parents of children who died by their own hands have seized the opportunity to lay the blame at someone else's doorstep—namely yours and mine. In the Judas Priest case, for one, there appeared to be a well-documented history of excessive behavior on the victim's part for some time prior to the suicide. Having failed to avoid or repair the damage, the parents hurried to blame a song, a lyric, or an imagined 'subliminal' message for the tragic state of their child's emotions. Is a lawsuit going to result from every suicide if the plaintiff needs only to name the last record the deceased heard?

Most parents understand that no results are guaranteed when raising children, but we can all safely assume that raising strong and well-motivated children requires a lot of dedication, support, love, patience, and hard work, and that when some of these items are missing from the family formula, the child will probably suffer negative consequences. We try to set good examples for our children, and to give them a strong set of values—tools for dealing with the world—and these values, together with our guidance and support, should be more than enough to allow them to withstand an entire universe of negative influences.

Don't blame rock'n'roll for your children's inability to cope. Blame yourself. Take a long, hard look in the mirror, admit your mistakes, and try to correct them. And consider those children, whose parents really do blame everybody but themselves; where were they headed after school? To a job? To the library? To a volunteer center? Is it surprising to find that many teenage suicide victims got high on a regular basis and performed poorly in both academics and extracurricular? Are these kids raised to be self-reliant, contributing members of society? Or are they left to themselves and to their own devices, with little parental guidance and even less positive input from their families?

The only thing I can be sure that I have in common with these bereaved parents is parenthood itself, and my kids have been raised on, in, and around hard rock music for their entire lives. They've literally grown up in a house where, among the more traditional types, the dinner guests have also included people like Ted Nugent, Dee Snider, Nikki Sixx, Tommy Lee, John Belushi, Billy Idol, Traci Guns, all the members of Poison . . . you get the picture. All three kids have been to concerts, they've all heard the four-letter chatter between songs, they've been backstage, they've all spent plenty of time in the studio, and they've been surrounded by hard rock lyrics virtually every day of their lives. The result?

Julia, 17, was president of the Student Council in her junior year of high school; she was chosen as one of twenty-five students to serve on the Mayor's Youth Advisory Council, she served as a phone counselor on the Cedars-Sinai Teen Line (for drug and suicide prevention), and currently is a peer educator at the Valley Community Clinic, counseling other teens when she's not at her after-school job. She sees, reads, and listens to what she feels merits her time or attention.

Nina, 14, is active in animal rights, wears no leather, has been a strict vegetarian for four years, is a working member of the Screen Actors Guild, and received an award from the East Valley Coordinating Committee for her volunteer work with young children at the library. Aside from maintaining a B average, she is a member of the school drill team and spends Sunday afternoons in acting class.

Daniel, 9, was chosen as an all-star on both his soccer and baseball teams. For the last six years, the kids have contributed to the cost of supporting our family's two foster children in Thailand through the Foster Parents Plan, and they write to them regularly.

I know Ted Nugent's children well; they are both fine kids, as are Rick Nielsen's two teenage boys. Ted raised his children from preschoolers by himself after the death of their mother. From the plaintiff parents' point of view in the Judas Priest suit, these children and mine (raised at the very core of depravity) should be disasters. Yet most of the children of the rock musicians I know are doing quite well, thank you.

Is heavy metal responsible for these results? Why am I compelled to tell you these things about my children, aside from the obvious pride I feel? It's not to prove that I'm a great dad, or that my wife is a great mom, or that our kids are better than *your* kids. No, this report card on my children is meant to illustrate that no amount of exposure to questionable influences is sufficient to alter the behavior of a child with a strong sense of values and of self.

If parents are mean to others, or to each other; if they drink heavily, if they abuse or mistreat their children or each other physically or emotionally, then the child will suffer the consequences. Those consequences may very well be tragic for that child, but most definitely *not* because he spent the morning listening to Ozzy or to Judas Priest.

ACKNOWLEDGMENTS

Thank you to Bud Karelis and Bob Bell for inspiration and counsel; Gregg Geller for amazing recall and fact-checking; Ed Tivnan for inspiration and organization; Bob Merlis for enthusiasm and advice; my editor Tom Seabrook for outstanding patience, verbal wisdom, and collaboration; my agent Lee Sobel for understanding my drift and quickly finding a home for it; my sound wizards Gary Ladinsky, Duane Baron, and Eddie Delena; my wife Suky and our children Julia, Nina, and Daniel for their love, support, and enduring tolerance for my questionable lifestyle; Andrew Hickey for his historical perspective on rock music; and Clive for giving me the opportunity of a lifetime.